# cooking
## on the coast

First published in 2008 by Murdoch Books Pty Limited as
Byron: cooking and eating. This edition published in 2011.

Murdoch Books Australia
Pier 8/9
23 Hickson Road
Millers Point NSW 2000
Phone: +61 (0) 2 8220 2000
Fax: +61 (0) 2 8220 2558
www.murdochbooks.com.au

Murdoch Books UK Limited
Erico House, 6th Floor
93–99 Upper Richmond Road
Putney, London SW15 2TG
Phone: +44 (0) 20 8785 5995
Fax: +44 (0) 20 8785 5985
www.murdochbooks.co.uk

For Corporate Orders & Custom Publishing, contact
Noel Hammond, National Development Manager.

Publisher: Kylie Walker
Photographer: Brett Boardman
Project manager: Gabriella Sterio
Editors: Jacqueline Blanchard and Desney King
Designer: MaryLouise Brammer
Cover Designer: Tania Gomes
Food editor: Jane Lawson
Stylist: Cherise Pagano (for pages 25, 30, 46, 85, 90,
109, 110, 127, 146, 184, 192, 195, 213, 214, 234)

National Library of Australia Cataloguing-in-Publication Data

Snow, Steven
Title: Cooking on the coast / Steven Snow.
Edition: 2nd ed.
ISBN: 978-1-74266-338-8
Notes: Includes index.
Subjects: Cooking. Byron Bay (NSW)
Dewey Number: 641.5

A catalogue record for this book is available from the British Library.

Printed by 1010 Printing International Limited in 2011. PRINTED IN CHINA.

IMPORTANT: Those who might be at risk from the effects of salmonella poisoning (the elderly,
pregnant women, young children and those suffering from immune deficiency diseases) should
consult their doctor with any concerns about eating raw eggs.

OVEN GUIDE: You may find cooking times vary depending on the oven you are using. For fan-forced
ovens, as a general rule, set the oven temperature to 20°C (35°F) lower than indicated in the recipe.

# cooking on the coast

steven snow

photographed by brett boardman

MURDOCH BOOKS

To Mum, Dad, Errol, Mitchell, Sammy, Mia, Darryl and Liane

# contents

# introduction

My intention in this book is to give away as many secrets and impart as much knowledge as I can about cooking with seafood and organic produce. It would be impossible to attempt this without also sharing the superb natural beauty and abundance of the New South Wales north coast where I have lived and worked for more than twenty years, and which has been pivotal in inspiring the way I live, cook and eat. Whether I am eating at my farm in Possum Creek, sharing a barbecue picnic with friends or cooking in the restaurant at Fins in Kingscliff, my cuisine is influenced by fishermen, surfing, wine, meditation, yoga, the exotic locations I have been to and the interesting people — from chefs to grandmothers — I have met along the way.

Early in my career I spent time working on a fishing boat and cooking in a seafood restaurant in France. I then travelled and worked in Portugal, where I learnt a lot about blending new and distinct flavours I had not encountered in Australia. I also came to appreciate the many ways local produce was used differently from region to region, depending on what was at hand. This, and a few remarkable forays through Asia, were pivotal in defining the direction of my food at Fins — peasant food embellished with fresh local produce.

While it would be ludicrous to suggest Fins is the best seafood restaurant in the world, my travels as a chef have made it clear, to me at least, that the far north coast of New South Wales has the best seafood I have encountered. At Fins, we serve line-caught local fish, prawns without chemicals and swimmingly fresh squid, bugs, crabs, scallops and octopus. The local produce we have on offer almost gives us an unfair advantage. As I say to my staff, 'If we get it wrong after this we should be shot!' When the produce is this good, it is very often what you don't do to it that makes the difference.

In this book I also want to share the flavours of my food and the colourful experience of running fine-dining regional restaurants in this amazing part of the world. I probably shouldn't mention (but will) what to do when snakes, sandflies, rats and mangoes impinge on the dining experience and how to respond when asked by a non-customer if they can leave a dead body in the outside dining area on a packed Friday night!

Strange encounters have always been the norm at Fins. One evening when we were still in Byron Bay a friendly guy called me to his table and mentioned he took the odd photograph. He enquired if I had published a cookbook. When I answered in the negative he suggested we get together and take a few shots. I later discovered he was at that time Australian Photographer of the Year. To say I enjoyed working with Brett Boardman would be a major understatement. He gets up too early, drinks my wine, eats my food — and I still love him!

The New South Wales north coast is unique and I cannot imagine a better area in which to run a restaurant. I hope you are inspired to reproduce some of these recipes at home. Don't feel as though you need to follow the recipes slavishly — taste and be led by your palate. After all, if it tastes good to you it will probably taste good to your guests!

# a note on food combining

Cooking with the best quality ingredients you can get (especially if they are organic) is going to improve any eating experience, but I also like to consider the science of food combining, or trophology, when I prepare a meal. I once read the headline, 'Top competitive eater gobbles down 44 lobsters in 12 minutes'. Apparently, this was after the woman had downed 35 bratwurst and over 21 grilled cheese sandwiches a week earlier to win $US50,000 on the American competitive eating circuit. Riveting stuff!

I am a big fan of trophology, which, simply put, means that combining certain types of food in a meal is complementary — they can be digested fully to provide our bodies with energy. This works on the premise that certain foods may oppose each other because they have different digestive requirements, thus wreaking havoc in our bodies. The basic rule is that proteins, such as meat, fish, eggs and nuts, should not be eaten at the same meal as carbohydrates, such as pasta, rice, bread and potatoes. So, for example, if you are going to eat a fish or steak (protein) meal, combine it with a salad or low-starch vegetable rather than potatoes or chips.

Some dietitians may scoff at the idea of food combining, but if, like me, you embrace this approach, it is easy to compose great meals even when dining out. At Fins all our meals have an accent on health, with the exception of our desserts. Having said that, there is no need to be a zealot about it — like all of life's greatest pleasures, moderation is the key.

You can bring this understanding to all your meals, so instead of eating a fish burger or a meat and salad sandwich, wrap the same contents in a lettuce leaf or sheets of nori. If you have a sweet tooth, enjoy your cake on its own, or after a salad, and skip the meat-and-potatoes main course. Don't follow a protein meal with fresh fruit as the fruit will sit in your stomach and ferment while waiting for the protein to digest.

Another food-combining guideline is to avoid extremely hot or cold liquids with foods. Rejoice in the fact that moderate amounts of wine or beer can aid digestion as they have already been fermented. Even the freshest, most wholesome foods go to waste when combined and consumed in ways that interfere with digestion. At least our lady lobster-eater consumed only one type of protein — even if she saw fit to do it 44 times.

# blissed out on the verandah

## dining in at Possum Creek

Restaurants are hot, busy, stressful, intense and noisy places. My country property is not. It is a quiet place where I am lucky enough to drink rainwater and breathe clean air and where my nearest neighbours are possums, koalas, wallabies and birdlife. The only noise is a permanently flowing creek — Possum Creek — a sound far gentler than the din of an exhaust fan.

Possum Creek allows me the opportunity to enjoy the absolute quiet and to lead a life without any of the usual aural clutter of televisions, traffic and other noise. It provides the balance — there is no better place than my front verandah to relax, enjoy and share good food with close friends.

One of my favourite things about cooking here is that I can enjoy a glass of wine at the same time. I do not follow the white wine with white meat and red wine with red meat adage — to me it is all about the weight of wine on the palate. I love chilled red wine and often recommend pinot noir due to its seafood-friendly palate, but here I have to admit a bias, as I would enjoy a chilled pinot noir with cornflakes!

When you are working in a busy restaurant, sleep deprivation is a way of life and running from appointments to work is the norm. To allow me to operate with a clear mind and maximum energy I have established a morning regime that involves fresh fruit, Qui Kung breathing, meditation and yoga. Meditation is essential. Shutting down my mind for a half-hour 'service' each day is a must. For me, it is the difference between having a mind filled with constant background static that limits understanding, and being clear and present for whatever the day brings. Qui Kung is a form of deep breathing learnt from the Chinese that 'awakens' the major body organs and charges the body with energy — a great way to start the day. It is purported to prevent disease, increase wellbeing and even enhance your sex life. I like the energy boost.

At Possum Creek, breakfast starts with fresh (as in straight from my garden or trees) citrus, berries or whatever fruit is in season. Lunch is also served from the garden and usually involves a combination of fresh herbs, tomatoes, lettuce, cucumbers and something from the Bangalow farmers market. Located just up the road, the market offers me the best fresh produce, filled with maximum enzymes and antioxidants, rather than the pot-luck of cold-stored and freighted offerings from the supermarket. When I'm at work I top up this healthy routine with a black coffee and a slice of chocolate chilli torte (see page 218). This diet keeps it all happening until after dinner service in the restaurant.

Long before I bought my property at Possum Creek, bunya nut trees were growing naturally on my acreage. In early February you can be lying in bed and hear the thud of the pandanus-like cones as they explode onto the ground after plummeting 30 metres. It is truly satisfying to collect produce from your own backyard and for this reason I have planted my property out with citrus fruits and vegetables that I can use in the kitchen from season to season.

You'd be surprised how resourceful you can be when you look over your garden. Even when banana trees are not fruiting, their verdant leaves are fantastic visual garnishes that can be used to serve meals on. But nothing beats pulling ripe bananas from the tree just outside your kitchen door and using them as the stars of a fabulous dessert. Some of my favourites to serve at home are banana fritters with kaffir lime and lemongrass syrup (see page 52) and a very memorable banana croissant pudding (see page 62).

As well as fruit and vegetables, a good herb garden is a necessity. No matter where you live you should be able to grow a few essential herbs. Even if you live in an apartment you can grow ornamental trees, such as bay and lemon myrtle — these not only look great in pots but can add a unique twist to a dish. Lemon myrtle has a natural affinity with seafood (see lemon myrtle king prawns with riesling and sour cream, page 24) but also complements any meat or vegetable dish. It can be used in cooking pasta, rice, vinaigrettes, chutneys, cheesecakes, lemonade and ice cream. I even use it in a pie with apple, polenta and golden syrup (see page 141).

While I was travelling through Portugal, Sunday lunch was ordained a necessity. It was customary for entire families to devote several hours to the ritual of eating and drinking together. Sitting around the dinner table and sharing meals in this way is great for nurturing relationships as well as satisfying the belly. In our time-poor society it may not be possible to eat every meal this way, but if you can try to do it at least once a week then everyone benefits. The recipes in this chapter are perfect for getting the conversation started.

Dining in restaurants is great but dinner parties on the verandah are surreal. Fish mixed with Possum Creek produce and a trip to my wine cellar is the only way I know to solve the world's problems. Throw in a warm night, stars shining in the sky and good company and I start to wonder whether it's ever worth leaving Possum Creek, even for a ticket to heaven.

## bay leaves

Bay trees look beautiful and their leaves feature in many of the Portuguese-inspired dishes at Fins. Bay leaves have digestive qualities and a pleasant pine-like smell. You can serve the leaves whole in a casserole or in a sauce for flavour and decoration. Add the leaves early in the cooking process to allow them time to work their magic, and remember to remove them before blending. Fresh and dried bay leaves are about as similar as fresh and tinned tuna! Fresh bay leaves have a far superior flavour and aroma, and they are stronger as well. You will need to use two dried bay leaves for every fresh leaf to create the same approximation of flavour.

# portuguese-style mussels with chorizo tomato sauce

40 black mussels
125 ml (4 fl oz/1/2 cup) extra virgin olive oil
1/2 brown onion, finely sliced
1 garlic clove, finely chopped
4 fresh bay leaves
200 g (7 oz) chorizo sausage, cut into 2 mm (1/16 inch) slices
250 ml (9 fl oz/1 cup) white wine
250 g (9 oz/1 cup) tomato sauce (Basics, see page 231)
steamed jasmine rice, to serve

Serves 4

Scrub the mussels with a stiff brush and pull out the hairy beards. Discard any broken mussels, or open ones that don't close when tapped on the work surface. Rinse well and drain.

Heat the oil in a large saucepan over high heat. Add the onion, garlic, bay leaves and chorizo and cook, stirring regularly, for 4 minutes, or until the onion is lightly golden. Add the mussels and cook for a further 2 minutes, then add the wine. Bring to a boil, then add the tomato sauce.

Cover the saucepan with a tight-fitting lid and steam, shaking the pan occasionally, for a further 5 minutes, or until the mussels open. Discard any mussels that do not open.

Serve the mussels and sauce in large bowls with steamed jasmine rice on the side.

## Bruny Island abalone

A few years back I went to Tasmania to cook at Barilla Bay Oyster Farm as a guest chef. While I was there a friend took me diving off Bruny Island in search of a bag limit of abalone. I had heard stories of pristine Tasmanian waters and was anticipating a beautiful countryside bathed in winter sun.

When we arrived it was freezing cold and the water was so murky that my friend, who is an experienced diver, was unsure if we should 'take the plunge'. I think the fact that Brett was in the boat, armed to take photos of the action, tipped the scales, and I soon found myself kitted up. I love diving and could not believe the size and number of abalone to be found among the bull kelp.

The next night, I cooked for a hundred people. At the end of the evening, while sharing a great Tasmanian pinot with a guest, I mentioned the diving adventure of the previous day. Part way through the story she sought clarification as to where we had actually dived. She mentioned that it is well known among locals as a breeding ground for white pointer sharks. I then understood my diving companion's reticence the day before and immediately confronted him, armed with this new information. My friend was alcohol-impaired and replied 'F—- Snowy, as if you would have gone in the water if I told you that!'

The next day we barbecued the abalone, and wow — it was better than fantastic!

Abalones are delicious sea snails that need to be cooked quickly after being bought (or caught, if you are lucky enough). In Australia they are farmed in Tasmania. They are best cooked Asian-style — in this recipe they take on the subtle flavours of the sauce to make a very special omelette.

## abalone with asian omelette

### filling

120 g (4¹/₄ oz) fresh abalone
2 tablespoons peanut oil
2 teaspoons sesame oil
1 garlic clove, finely chopped
1 cm (¹/₂ inch) piece ginger, finely chopped
2 teaspoons finely chopped long red chilli, (optional)
2 baby bok choy, leaves separated
8 oyster mushrooms, sliced
1 tablespoon fish sauce
1 tablespoon oyster sauce
1 tablespoon kecap manis
80 ml (2¹/₂ fl oz/¹/₃ cup) chicken stock (Basics, see page 230)

### omelette

2 eggs
1 teaspoon palm sugar (jaggery)
2 teaspoons fish sauce
2 tablespoons peanut oil
1 teaspoon sesame oil
12 coriander (cilantro) leaves, finely chopped
8 basil leaves, torn
1 small handful bean shoots
1 handful rocket (arugula) leaves, to garnish

Serves 4

Prepare the fresh abalone by removing the meat from the shell with a sharp knife. Wash the meat under cold running water, rubbing well to remove any dark-coloured slime. Trim off the digestive tract or the hard frilly edge — you can ask your fishmonger to do this for you. Gently pound the meat with a mallet on both sides to tenderise it, but be careful not to break the flesh. Cut the flesh into 5 mm (¹/₄ inch) thick slices.

To make the filling, heat the peanut and sesame oils in a wok over high heat, swirling to coat the base and sides. Add the garlic, ginger and chilli, and stir-fry for 30 seconds. Add the bok choy and mushrooms and stir-fry for 2 minutes. Add the sauces and stock and cook for 30 seconds, then add the abalone and cook for a further 30 seconds, or until heated through. Be careful not to overcook the abalone or it will be tough. Remove from the heat and set aside, reserving a little of the abalone to use as a garnish.

To make the omelettes, whisk together the eggs, palm sugar and fish sauce in a bowl until the sugar dissolves. Heat the peanut and sesame oils in a wok over high heat. Pour in a quarter of the egg mixture and spread it to create a circle with a 10 cm (4 inch) diameter. Cook the egg for 30 seconds, or until golden around the rim — it should still be a little uncooked in the centre. Scatter a quarter of the coriander, basil, bean shoots and abalone mix in the centre of the omelette and gently fold in half using a spatula. After a few seconds, remove the omelette and keep warm in a low oven. Repeat this process to create three more omelettes.

Serve each omelette with the pan juices drizzled over the top and fresh rocket leaves on the side. Garnish with the reserved abalone.

Lemon myrtle is to me what lemongrass is to other cooks. It is also seven times stronger. Even so, it adds a subtle, rather than overpowering, lemon flavour. Lemon myrtle may be used fresh or dried; you can use it as you would a bay leaf in recipes that require a lemony flavour, and substitute it in any recipe calling for lemongrass. In this dish it adds a latent background lemon exotica.

## lemon myrtle king prawns with riesling and sour cream

### lemon myrtle stock
250 ml (9 fl oz/1 cup) chicken stock
    (Basics, see page 130)
125 ml (4 fl oz/1/2 cup) riesling
3 lemon myrtle leaves or 1 lemongrass
    stem, bruised
white pepper, to taste
1 tablespoon butter
1 tablespoon plain (all-purpose) flour

60 ml (2 fl oz/1/4 cup) olive oil
1 garlic clove, finely chopped
16 large king prawns (shrimp), peeled
    and deveined, tails left intact
200 ml (7 fl oz) riesling
2 tablespoons sour cream (optional)

Serves 4

To make the lemon myrtle stock, put the chicken stock, wine and lemon myrtle leaves in a saucepan over medium–high heat. Bring to the boil then reduce the heat and add sea salt and white pepper, to taste. Simmer for 10 minutes. Remove from the heat and allow to stand for 10 minutes for the flavours to infuse.

Melt the butter in a large saucepan over medium–high heat and stir in the flour until smooth. Gradually whisk in the stock, until the liquid has a thick pouring consistency. Remove from the heat and pass through a sieve to remove any lumps. Set aside.

Heat the olive oil in a frying pan over medium heat. Add the garlic and prawns and cook for about 2 minutes, or until the prawns turn pink and start to curl. Add the wine to the pan and bring to the boil for 1 minute, or until the liquid has reduced by half. Add the lemon myrtle stock and sour cream, if desired, and bring the sauce back to the boil. Remove the prawns from the pan and place on a serving plate. Keep warm. Continue cooking the sauce for 2 minutes, or until slightly thickened.  Season with sea salt, to taste. Divide the prawns between serving plates and drizzle with the sauce.

These are not your average fish cakes — the reason they stand out is their texture and the inclusion of fresh herbs. They make a great appetiser and also work well on a shared table.

# snapper cakes

500 g (1 lb 2 oz) skinless, boneless snapper fillets
100 g (3¹/₂ oz/³/₄ cup) green beans,
    finely chopped
1 carrot, very finely chopped
2 garlic cloves, finely chopped
1.5 cm (⁵/₈ inch) piece ginger, finely chopped
1 lemongrass stem, white part only,
    very finely chopped
2 tablespoons sweet chilli sauce
¹/₂ bunch coriander (cilantro), finely chopped
¹/₂ bunch basil, finely chopped
1 tablespoon caster (superfine) sugar
10 drops fish sauce
2 makrut (kaffir lime) leaves, finely chopped
plain (all-purpose) flour, for dusting
davidson's plum chutney (Basics, see page 223),
    to serve

Makes 16

Put the fish into a food processor and process for 3 minutes, or until you have small even chunks (do not over-process into a paste, as these cakes should have a bit of texture). Transfer the fish to a bowl and add the chopped beans, carrot, garlic, ginger, lemongrass, sweet chilli sauce, coriander, basil, sugar, fish sauce and makrut leaves. Mix together to thoroughly combine.

Take 1 tablespoonful of mixture at a time and use your hands to roll a neat ball. Flatten slightly with the palm of your hand and place on a tray. Repeat with the remaining mixture — you should make 16 balls in total. Cover with plastic wrap and refrigerate for 1–2 hours.

Fill a deep-fryer or large heavy-based saucepan one-third full of oil and heat to 180°C (350°F). Lightly dust the snapper cakes in flour and deep-fry them, in batches, for about 3 minutes each, or until golden and crispy. Drain on paper towels.

Serve hot with davidson's plum chutney on the side for dipping.

note You can also pan-fry these snapper cakes lightly in oil, or cook on a barbecue plate, for 2 minutes each side, or until golden and cooked through.

## peruvian-style corn with bugs and lime butter

16 x 100 g (3¹/₂ oz) Moreton Bay or Balmain
    bugs (marron or crayfish can be used
    as a substitute)
2 whole corn cobs, with husks
1 tablespoon caster (superfine) sugar
80 ml (2¹/₂ fl oz/¹/₃ cup) freshly squeezed
    lime juice
100 ml (3¹/₂ fl oz) extra virgin olive oil
60 g (2¹/₄ oz) butter
lemon wedges, to serve

Serves 4

Cut each bug in half lengthways and remove the
intestinal tract.

Put the corn (with husks on) into a large saucepan
with 4 litres (140 fl oz/16 cups) cold water and
1 tablespoon of sea salt. Add the sugar and half
the lime juice and bring to a boil. Reduce the heat
and simmer for 10 minutes, or until the corn husk is
soft and the kernels tender. Drain and allow to cool
slightly, then remove and discard the husks. Cut
each corn cob into halves lengthways, and place
one half on each serving plate.

Heat some of the olive oil in a frying pan over
medium–high heat. Working in batches, add the
bugs, cut side down, and cook for 1 minute, then
add some of the butter and a little lime juice to
the pan. Season with sea salt, to taste. Cook for
2–3 minutes, or until the bug meat is opaque.
Repeat until all the bug halves are cooked.

To serve, place the bugs on top of the corn and
drizzle over the pan juices. Garnish with a lemon
wedge for squeezing over.

Moreton Bay bugs may look like they come from another planet but they are simple earthlings found in abundance in the shallow waters on the far north coast of New South Wales and in southern Queensland, where they are caught year-round. When cooked, these frill-necked orange creatures have a firm, sweet meat — they also look great served on platters.

# tuna with tamarind sauce

4 x 165 g (5³/₄ oz) sashimi-grade tuna steaks
250 ml (9 fl oz/1 cup) Asian marinade
     (Basics, see page 222)

(Basics, see page 222)

### tamarind sauce
80 ml (2¹/₂ fl oz/¹/₃ cup) peanut oil
1 tablespoon sesame oil
1 tablespoon palm sugar (jaggery)
1 brown onion, finely sliced
2 garlic cloves, finely chopped
1.5 cm (⁵/₈ inch) piece ginger, finely chopped
1 tablespoon coriander (cilantro) root, chopped
1 tablespoon fish sauce
80 ml (2¹/₂ fl oz/¹/₃ cup) shaoxing rice wine
1 tablespoon Chinese sweet black vinegar
60 g (2¹/₄ oz/¹/₄ cup) tamarind purée

500 ml (17 fl oz/2 cups) chicken stock (Basics,
     see page 230)
1 teaspoon dark soy sauce

100 g (3¹/₂ oz/1 cup) snow peas (mangetout),
     trimmed
1 red capsicum (pepper), seeded, membrane
     removed and finely sliced
50 g (1³/₄ oz) mixed shiitake and enoki
     mushrooms
steamed Asian greens, to serve

Serves 4

Put the Asian marinade in a shallow baking dish and add the tuna steaks, turning to coat all over. Set aside for 10 minutes to marinate.

Meanwhile, make the tamarind sauce. Heat the peanut and sesame oils in a saucepan over medium–high heat. Add the palm sugar and cook for 1 minute, or until melted. Add the onion, garlic, ginger and coriander root and cook for 5 minutes, or until the onions are lightly golden. Add the fish sauce, rice wine, vinegar and tamarind purée and bring to the boil. Cook for 2 minutes, then add the chicken stock. Reduce the heat and simmer for 20 minutes, or until reduced by one-third. Stir in the soy sauce, then remove from the heat and strain the sauce through a fine sieve.

Return to the warm saucepan and bring to a simmer. Add the snow peas, capsicum and mushrooms and bring to the boil. Reduce the heat and simmer for 1 minute, or until the vegetables are tender. Remove from the heat and keep warm until ready to serve.

Preheat a chargrill pan or barbecue chargrill plate to high and sear the tuna for 1 minute, brushing both sides with the marinade. Turn over and cook for a further 1 minute, so the tuna is still pink in the middle. Remove from the heat.

Place each tuna steak over a bed of steamed Asian greens. Arrange the vegetables on top and drizzle with the tamarind sauce, to serve.

# spanner crab chowder

600 g (1 lb 5 oz) whole cooked spanner
    crab or mud crab
100 g (3¹/₂ oz) butter
2 brown onions, finely sliced
4 garlic cloves, finely chopped
2 small all-purpose potatoes, such as
    pontiacs, peeled and finely sliced
10 anchovy fillets
750 ml (26 fl oz/3 cups) chicken or fish
    stock (Basics, see page 230)
sour cream, to serve (optional)

Serves 4

To remove the meat from the crab, lift the small flap on the underside of the crab and prise off the top hard shell. Remove the soft internal organs and pull off the grey feathery gills. Using a large sharp knife, cut the crab lengthways through the centre of the body, forming two halves with the legs attached. Cut the crab in half again, crossways. Crack the claws with the back of a cleaver and gently remove the meat from the body and claws. Refrigerate until ready to use.

Melt the butter in a saucepan over medium heat. Add the onion, garlic, potato slices and anchovies and cook for 8 minutes, or until the potato is softened slightly. Season with 2 pinches sea salt and a pinch of cracked black pepper. Add the stock and stir. Bring to the boil, then reduce the heat and simmer for 45 minutes, or until the potato is very tender. Remove from the heat and allow to cool slightly before transferring to a food processor and blending until just smooth. Adjust the seasoning, to taste.

Reserve some of the crabmeat to use as a garnish and divide the rest in the bottom of four soup bowls. Ladle the soup into each bowl and add a drizzle of sour cream, if desired. Decorate with the reserved crabmeat and serve.

# barbecue chilli fish

100 ml (3¹/₂ fl oz) extra virgin olive oil
1 fresh small red chilli, very finely chopped
2 cm (³/₄ inch) piece ginger, very finely chopped
2 garlic cloves, finely chopped
2 kg (4 lb 8 oz) whole snapper, cleaned and scaled
1¹/₂ tablespoons freshly squeezed lime juice
green salad, to serve

Serves 2

To make the marinade, mix the oil, chilli and
ginger together in a bowl until well combined.

Grind the garlic and some sea salt to make a
soft paste.

Cut two parallel lines along the length of the fish
through to the bone — this will stop the fish
curling during cooking. Cut another two parallel
lines from the bottom of the fish to the top to
make a noughts and crosses pattern over the fish.
Repeat on the other side.

Rub the garlic paste evenly over the fish, making
sure the paste fills the cuts on both sides. Brush
the marinade over the fish.

Preheat the barbecue grill plate to high and cook
the fish for 4 minutes on each side, continuing
to brush the marinade over the fish as it cooks,
until the flesh starts to turn opaque near the bone
when checked with a sharp knife.

Just before taking the fish off the barbecue,
season with the lime juice. Serve with a fresh
green salad.

## bunya nuts

Bunya nut season runs from February to March and, as far as I'm concerned, deserves a bit of celebration. Remove the nuts from their cones, boil in water for 30 minutes, then turn off the heat and leave them to cool in the water. Cut the nuts in half lengthways and remove them from the brown shells. Heat some olive oil in a frying pan with a bit of sea salt and cook the nuts for about 5 minutes or until golden. They are delicious with a cold beer.

This recipe showcases the Australian bunya nut. The chestnut-flavoured nuts are mixed into a paste I learnt from an old man in Indonesia. The paste tastes amazing stuffed in squid, chargrilled and served in this Asian-inspired sauce.

## bunya nut stuffed squid

### stuffing

60 ml (2¼ fl oz/¼ cup) peanut oil
1 tablespoon sesame oil
2 brown onions, sliced
2 tablespoons Fins shrimp paste (Basics, see page 223)
4 garlic cloves, crushed
1.5 cm (⅝ inch) piece ginger, finely chopped
2 tablespoons kecap manis
400 g (14 oz/2 cups) steamed jasmine rice
4 anchovy fillets
40 g (1½ oz/¼ cup) bunya nuts or toasted macadamia nuts
40 g (1½ oz/¼ cup) peanuts

### sauce

1 teaspoon sesame oil
2 tablespoons peanut oil
½ brown onion, cut into 1.5 cm (⅝ inch) pieces
1 teaspoon Fins shrimp paste (Basics, see page 223)
2 garlic cloves, chopped
1 cm (½ inch) piece ginger, finely chopped
2 tablespoons kecap manis
2 tablespoons fish sauce
685 ml (23½ fl oz/2¾ cups) chicken stock (Basics, see page 230)
½ red capsicum (pepper), seeded, membrane removed and cut into 1.5 cm (⅝ inch) pieces
1 makrut (kaffir lime) leaf, finely sliced

24 small cleaned squid tubes (see note)
steamed jasmine rice, to serve

Serves 8

To make the stuffing, heat the peanut and sesame oils in a frying pan over medium heat. Add the onion and cook for 5 minutes, or until soft but not coloured. Add the shrimp paste, garlic and ginger and cook for 3 minutes, or until lightly golden. Add the kecap manis and steamed rice. Continue to cook for 5 minutes, stirring often. Remove from the heat and allow to cool.

To make the sauce, heat the sesame and peanut oils in a saucepan. Add the onion and cook for 5 minutes, or until softened. Add the shrimp paste, garlic and ginger and cook for 3 minutes, or until golden. Add the kecap manis, fish sauce and stock and bring to a boil. Skim any foam from the top and simmer for 10 minutes, then add the capsicum and continue simmering for 5 minutes further, or until softened. Add the lime leaf to the hot sauce. Keep warm until ready to serve. Preheat the oven to 150°C (300°F/Gas 2).

Transfer the rice stuffing to a food processor. Add the anchovies, bunya nuts and peanuts and blend until smooth. Put the stuffing in a piping bag and pipe the mixture into the cleaned squid tubes, securing the openings with a toothpick.

Preheat the barbecue grill plate to medium. Chargrill the stuffed squid tubes for 3 minutes, turning once, until coloured all over. Transfer to a baking tray and bake in the oven for 5 minutes, or until the filling is heated through. Serve the squid tubes with steamed jasmine rice and drizzle the sauce over the top.

note If you are preparing the squid tubes from scratch, hold the squid in both hands, then pull the head and tentacles from the body. Remove the internal organs from the body and rinse under running water, making sure you remove the transparent quill. With your fingers, pull the skin from the body and discard.

## beetroot and pinot risotto with king prawns

250 ml (9 fl oz/1 cup) extra virgin olive oil
4 tablespoons butter
1 brown onion, finely sliced
2 garlic cloves, finely chopped
4 anchovy fillets, chopped
1 fresh bay leaf
325 g (11 1/2 oz/1 1/2 scant cups) arborio rice
250 ml (9 fl oz/1 cup) pinot noir
6 whole beetroot (beets), juiced
1 litre (35 fl oz/4 cups) chicken stock (Basics, see page 230)
36 raw king prawns (shrimp), peeled and deveined, tails left intact
200 ml (7 fl oz) dry white wine
2 tablespoons finely chopped parsley
200 g (7 oz/4 cups) baby English spinach leaves, steamed, to serve
185 ml (6 fl oz/3/4 cup) saffron mayonnaise (Basics, see page 229), to serve

Serves 6

To make the beetroot and pinot risotto, heat 100 ml (3½ fl oz) of the olive oil with 2 tablespoons of the butter in a saucepan over medium–high heat. Add the onion, garlic, anchovies and bay leaf and cook for 8–10 minutes, or until golden. Add the rice and stir to coat in the oil. Add ½ cup of the pinot noir and stir constantly until absorbed. Repeat with the remaining wine and stir in half the beetroot juice. When almost all the liquid is absorbed, add the chicken stock and remaining beetroot juice a little at a time, allowing almost all the liquid to be absorbed before each new addition. Season with sea salt and cracked black pepper, to taste. Continue cooking, stirring until the rice is tender and most of the liquid has been absorbed — the whole process should take about 25 minutes.

Meanwhile, heat the remaining olive oil in a large frying pan over high heat. Add the prawns and cook for 1 minute on each side, or until they turn pink and start to curl. Season with sea salt, then add the white wine, cooking until almost all the wine has been absorbed. Add the remaining butter to the pan and cook for 1 minute, stirring to coat. Add the parsley and stir through just before you are ready to serve.

To serve, place a mound of risotto on individual plates (you can use a small ramekin as a mould — just wet it with a bit of hot water first so the rice doesn't stick). Arrange the prawns and steamed spinach around the risotto and drizzle any remaining pan juices over the top. Garnish with a dollop of saffron mayonnaise.

### farmers market
Every Tuesday I head for New Brighton Farmers Market where I buy supplies for home and the fresh produce for Fins. The farmers love it when I arrive, as cartons of blueberries, eggs, green papaya, lemons and limes (when the ones from Possum Creek are all used up) are ferried to the car. Farmers markets and roadside stalls are the best way to shop for your local economy, your health and the environment.

I first cooked this meal in the Alentejo region of Portugal where I was staying in a 19th-century B&B called Herdade da Matinha. This dish really brings out the best of Portuguese flavours and is in complete harmony with either a red wine from the Douro Valley in Portugal, or an aged semillon from the Hunter Valley.

## baked snapper with garlic and smoked paprika crust

1 kg (2 lb 4 oz) whole snapper, cleaned
    and scaled
5 garlic cloves, peeled
1 tablespoon butter
1½ teaspoons smoked paprika
300 g (10½ oz/1¼ scant cups) tinned
    chopped tomatoes
3 tablespoons finely chopped Italian
    (flat-leaf) parsley
150 ml (5 fl oz) olive oil
2 large brown onions, sliced into rings
500 g (1 lb 2 oz) new potatoes, peeled
250 ml (9 fl oz/1 cup) dry white wine

Serves 2

Preheat the oven to 180°C (350°F/Gas 4).

On each side of the snapper, make three diagonal cuts through the thickest part of the fish to the bone. Then, using a large mortar and pestle, crush together the garlic, butter, 1 teaspoon paprika and 1 teaspoon sea salt. Add the tomatoes and parsley and crush to create a paste. Season with cracked black pepper, to taste. Rub the paste all over the fish, ensuring the cuts and stomach cavity are well coated.

Put the olive oil and onions in a shallow roasting tin and place the fish on top. Arrange the potatoes around the fish and scatter with sea salt. Bake in the oven for 10 minutes. Pour the wine over the fish, return to the oven and bake for a further 10 minutes, or until just cooked, basting often with the pan juices until the flesh is opaque — it should flake easily with a fork when pressed into the widest part of the fish.

Serve the fish and potatoes straight from the oven or arrange on a platter.

# beer-battered fish and chips

800 g (1 lb 12 oz) floury potatoes, such as russet (idaho) or sebago
125 g (4$^1$/$_2$ oz/1 cup) self-raising flour
125 ml (4 fl oz/$^1$/$_2$ cup) iced water
60 ml (2 fl oz/$^1$/$_4$ cup) beer
a pinch turmeric or curry powder (optional), plus extra for dusting
4 x 150 g (5$^1$/$_2$ oz) boneless, skinless fish fillets, such as flathead, snapper, jewfish or leatherjacket, cut into quarters lengthways
white pepper, to taste
vegetable oil, for deep-frying
flour, for dusting
lemon or lime wedges, to serve

Serves 4

Peel and cut the potatoes into chips about 2 cm (3/4 inch) thick and pat dry with paper towels or a clean tea towel (dish towel).

Fill a deep-fryer or large heavy-based saucepan one-third full of oil and heat to 150°C (300°F). Cook the chips, in batches, for 8–10 minutes, or until pale golden. Remove from the oil and drain on paper towels. Increase the heat so that the oil reaches a temperature of 180°C (350°F). Return the chips to the pan for a further 3–4 minutes, or until brown and crisp on the outside. Remove from the oil and drain on paper towels. Season with sea salt and cracked black pepper. Keep warm in a medium oven.

To make the batter, put the flour, iced water, beer and turmeric in a bowl and whisk until smooth.

Season the fish with sea salt. Roll the fish in the flour to coat, and then dip in the batter until covered, shaking off any excess. Deep-fry the fish fillets for 2 minutes each, or until golden (the fish pieces will float when cooked). Remove from the oil and drain on paper towels. Serve immediately with the chips and lemon or lime wedges for squeezing over.

note Be careful when deep-frying the chips as water from the potatoes causes the oil to rise when the chips are added.

# red curry with king prawns

200 ml (7 fl oz) fish or chicken stock (Basics, see page 230)
4 fresh or dried lemon myrtle leaves or 1 lemongrass stem, white part only
1 1/2 tablespoons peanut oil
1 teaspoon sesame oil
1 garlic clove, finely chopped
5 mm (1/4 inch) piece of ginger, finely chopped
1 tablespoon red curry paste (Basics, see page 228)
24 large raw king prawns (shrimp), peeled and deveined, tails left intact
2 tablespoons fish sauce
1 tablespoon kecap manis
80 ml (2 1/2 fl oz/1/3 cup) coconut milk
12 basil leaves
12 coriander (cilantro) leaves
steamed jasmine rice, to serve (optional)

Serves 4

Heat the stock in a saucepan over medium–high heat and add the lemon myrtle leaves or lemongrass. Bring to the boil, then reduce the heat and simmer for 10 minutes to allow the flavours to infuse..

Heat the peanut and sesame oils in a wok over high heat, swirling to coat the base and sides. Add the garlic, ginger and curry paste and cook for 2 minutes, or until aromatic. Add the prawns and stir to coat, then add the fish sauce and kecap manis, tossing to coat the prawns. Add the stock and bring to the boil, then reduce to a simmer for 1 minute. Add the coconut milk and bring back to the boil, then remove from the heat. Add the basil and coriander and stir through. Serve immediately with steamed jasmine rice, if desired.

To me, Tasmania is the 'produce isle'. It was here I was first introduced to 'stripey' — a firm, fatty and tasty cold-water fish. It is my personal favourite non-north coast fish.

# striped trumpeter with wasabi mash and sautéed spinach

### wasabi mash
850 g (1 lb 14 oz) all-purpose potatoes,
    such as desirée
1 tablespoon dried wasabi powder
250 ml (9 fl oz/1 cup) milk
100 g (3½ oz) butter

### sautéed spinach
60 ml (2 fl oz/¼ cup) olive oil
1 garlic clove, finely sliced
500 g (1 lb 2 oz) baby English spinach leaves

### striped trumpeter
4 x 160 g (5¾ oz) striped trumpeter fillets
    (snapper, jewfish or blue-eye trevalla
    can be used as a substitute)
white pepper, to taste
plain (all-purpose) flour, for dusting
100 ml (3½ fl oz) olive oil
125 ml (4 fl oz/½ cup) dry white wine
3 tablespoons freshly squeezed lemon juice
1 tablespoon butter

Serves 4

To make the wasabi mash, peel and cut the potatoes into quarters and steam them for about 20 minutes, or until soft (by steaming, the potatoes take on less water than boiling). Put the potatoes through a mouli, if you have one, or mash well with a potato masher (do not use a food processor or the potato will become glue-like).

In a separate bowl, mix the wasabi powder with about 2 tablespoons water to form a thick paste. Heat the milk and butter in a saucepan and stir until the butter has melted. Mix the combined milk, butter and wasabi into the mashed potatoes, beating with a spoon until as smooth as possible. Season with sea salt and cracked black pepper, to taste, then cover and keep warm.

Preheat the oven to 180°C (350°F/Gas 4). Season the fish fillets with sea salt and white pepper and dust lightly in the flour.

To make the sautéed spinach, heat the olive oil in a frying pan over high heat. Add the garlic and spinach and cook for 1 minute, or until wilted. Season with sea salt, to taste. Set aside and cover to keep warm.

To cook the fish, heat the olive oil in a large frying pan over medium heat and add the fish fillets. Cook for 2 minutes on each side, or until golden. Remove the fish from the pan, transfer them to a baking tray, place in the oven and cook for a further 3 minutes.

While the fish is baking, add the white wine, lemon juice and butter to the pan with the juices from the fish and stir, scraping the bottom of the pan to lift off any residue. Bring to the boil and cook for 3 minutes, or until slightly thickened.

Divide the mash among four plates, then place four equal portions of spinach on top. When the fish is cooked, lay it over the spinach. Drizzle a small amount of the sauce over the fish and serve immediately.

Fantastic gastronomic experiences are all too rare in life. I had one eating this pizza with a bottle of calabrese in a small Italian restaurant built into the side of a cliff in Taormina, Sicily. Pizza need not be laden with toppings — this was the pizza of my life!

## pizza trocadero

### pizza base
125 ml (4 fl oz/1/2 cup) milk
1 tablespoon active dried yeast
440 g (151/2 oz/31/2 cups) plain (all-purpose) flour
2 tablespoons extra virgin olive oil
1 teaspoon honey

200 g (7 oz) very ripe Roma (plum) tomatoes,
    crushed by hand
200 g (7 oz/11/3 cups) mozzarella cheese,
    roughly torn
12 slices prosciutto, chopped
1 small oregano sprig, leaves chopped
50 g (13/4 oz/11/3 cups) rocket (arugula) leaves
50 g (13/4 oz/1/2 cup) shaved parmesan cheese
extra virgin olive oil, to serve

Makes 4 small pizzas

To make the pizza bases, put the milk in a bowl with 125 ml (4 fl oz/1/2 cup) water. Add the yeast and stir until dissolved. Add 2 tablespoons of flour and mix to combine. Cover with plastic wrap and leave to stand in a warm place for 20 minutes, or until the mixture is foamy.

Pour the remaining flour into a stainless-steel bowl and make a well in the centre. Add the yeast mix, oil, honey and 1/2 teaspoon sea salt. Combine well and gather into a ball. Knead on a lightly floured surface for 15 minutes until smooth and elastic. Divide the dough into four equal portions, cover with a tea towel (dish towel) and allow to rest in a warm place for 1 hour, or until the dough doubles in size.

Preheat the oven to 220°C (425°F/Gas 7). Lightly grease four 20 cm (8 inch) round pizza trays. Roll each portion of dough evenly into a round crust that is 3 mm (1/8 inch) thick and large enough to fit the pizza trays, trimming to fit if necessary. Bake each base in the oven for about 5 minutes, or until lightly golden. Remove from the oven and allow to cool.

Increase the oven temperature to 250°C (500°F/Gas 9). Arrange the tomato, mozzarella, prosciutto and oregano over each pizza base. Cook in the oven for 8–10 minutes, or until the cheese is melted and bubbling. Remove from the oven and sprinkle with the fresh rocket leaves and parmesan cheese. Drizzle with olive oil, cut into slices and serve.

## seafood pescador with pasta

8 black mussels or pipis
4 Moreton Bay or Balmain bugs
400 g (14 oz) boneless, skinless white fish fillets, such as mahi mahi, kingfish, blue-eye trevalla or leatherjacket
4 cleaned squid tubes, cut into 2 cm (3/4 inch) squares
8 large raw king prawns (shrimp), peeled and deveined, tails left intact
500 g (1 lb 2 oz) fettuccini or spaghetti

### pescador sauce
200 ml (7 fl oz) extra virgin olive oil
2 onions, finely sliced
1 garlic clove, crushed
6 anchovy fillets, chopped
1 fresh bay leaf
1 tablespoon lisbon paste (Basics, see page 226)
250 ml (9 fl oz/1 cup) white wine
500 g (1 lb 2 oz/2 cups) tinned chopped tomatoes
1 teaspoon sugar
185 g (61/2 oz/3/4 cup) sour cream (optional)
18 pitted kalamata olives, halved

Serves 4

Scrub the mussels with a stiff brush and pull out the hairy beards. Discard any broken mussels, or open ones that don't close when tapped on the work surface. Rinse well. Remove the heads from the bugs, then cut them in half lengthways. Cut the fish fillets into 18 pieces that are just larger than bite-sized.

To make the pescador sauce, heat the oil in a large frying pan over high heat. Add the onion, garlic, anchovies and bay leaf and cook for 5 minutes, or until the onion has softened. Add the lisbon paste and cook for 1 minute. Add the wine and bring to the boil, then stir in the tomatoes and sugar and season with sea salt and cracked black pepper, to taste. Reduce the heat to low, cover, and simmer for 15 minutes.

Add the mussels to the pan and cook for about 3 minutes, then add the bugs and fish and cook for 2 minutes or until they turn opaque. Add the squid and prawns and cook for a further 2 minutes, or until the prawns turn pink and start to curl. Discard any unopened mussels. Add the olives and sour cream, if desired, just before serving, stirring to combine well. Season, to taste.

Meanwhile, cook the spaghetti in a saucepan of salted boiling water according to the manufacturer's instructions until al dente. Remove from the heat and drain well.

Toss the pasta through the sauce to combine and serve immediately.

# banana fritters with kaffir lime and lemongrass syrup

### lime and lemongrass syrup

1 lemongrass stem, lightly bruised
5 fresh kaffir lime (makrut) leaves
250 g (9 oz/1 heaped cup) caster (superfine)
    sugar
3 tablespoons honey
1 vanilla bean, split lengthways
2 cardamom pods, crushed
a dash of lime juice

### banana fritters

175 g (6 oz/1 cup) rice flour
55 g (2 oz/$^1$/$_4$ cup) caster (superfine) sugar
a pinch bicarbonate of soda (baking soda)
1 egg, lightly beaten
250 ml (9 fl oz/1 cup) milk
4 firm bananas (sugar or lady fingers are best)
plain (all-purpose) flour, for dusting
vegetable oil, for deep-frying
110 g (3$^3$/$_4$ oz/$^1$/$_2$ cup) caster (superfine) sugar
    combined with 1 teaspoon ground cinnamon,
    for dusting
vanilla ice cream (Basics, see page 225), to serve
    (optional)

Serves 4

To make the lime and lemongrass syrup, put the lemongrass, kaffir lime, sugar, honey, vanilla bean, cardamom and lime juice in a saucepan over medium–high heat. Add 300 ml (10$^1$/$_2$ fl oz) water and stir until the sugar has dissolved, then reduce the heat and simmer for 10 minutes, or until the liquid is reduced by half. Use a fine sieve to strain. The syrup can be served hot or cold; if you want to serve it warm, keep warm over a low heat, otherwise, remove from the heat and set aside until you are ready to serve.

To make the banana fritters, combine the rice flour, sugar and bicarbonate of soda in a bowl. Add the egg, milk and a pinch of salt and whisk until the batter is smooth. Cut the bananas into 2.5 cm (1 inch) thick diagonal slices.

Fill a deep-fryer or large heavy-based saucepan one-third full of oil and heat to 180°C (350°F). Lightly dust the banana slices in flour and then dip into the batter, shaking off any excess. Deep-fry the bananas, in batches, for about 2 minutes each, or until golden and crispy. Drain on paper towels. Repeat with the remaining banana slices.

Roll the fried banana fritters in the cinnamon sugar to coat while they are still warm and serve with the syrup and vanilla ice cream, if desired.

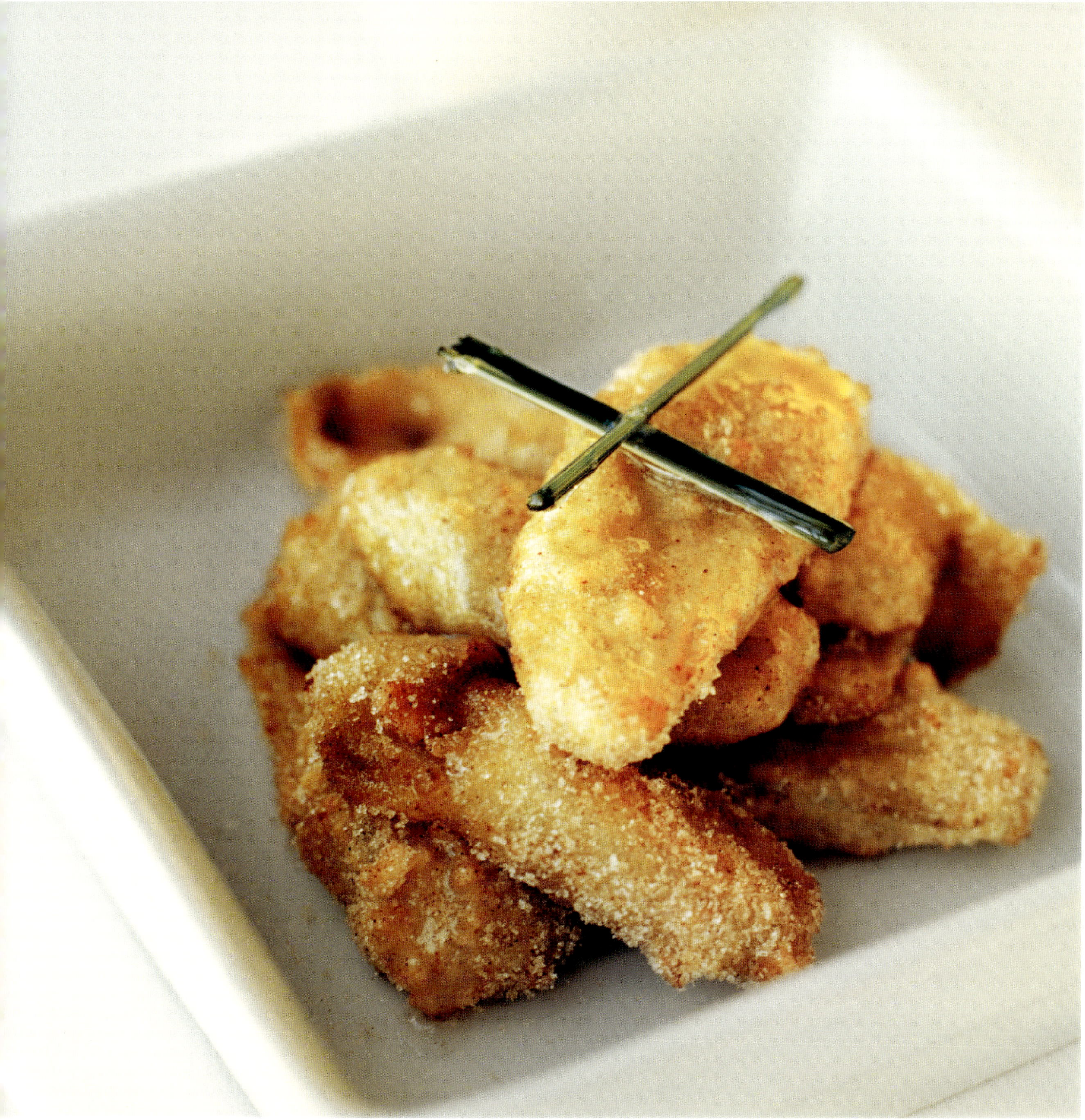

This Spanish rice pudding with sherry is the best kind of comfort food and even better with a rich, mouth-filling chocolatey sherry. Pedro Ximénez grapes are laid on bamboo mats to dry in the sun before being introduced to oak barrels for further maturation — it's the perfect sherry to drink with this dish.

## arroz con leche

750 ml (26 fl oz/3 cups) milk
1 cinnamon stick
1 vanilla bean, split lengthways, seeds scraped
3 strips lemon zest, white pith removed
140 g (5 oz/2/3 cup) short-grain white rice
3 egg yolks, lightly beaten
115 g (4 oz/1/3 cup) golden syrup (dark corn syrup)
60 g (2 1/4 oz) unsalted butter
125 ml (4 fl oz/1/2 cup) Pedro Ximénez sherry, or
    other rich dark sherry
stewed rhubarb or seasonal fruit, to serve
    (optional)

Serves 4

Put the milk, cinnamon, vanilla bean and seeds, lemon zest and a pinch of salt in a large saucepan over medium–high heat and bring almost to the boil. Reduce the heat to low and simmer for 2 minutes. Remove from the heat and set aside for 10 minutes to allow the flavours to infuse. Strain the liquid back into a clean saucepan and bring back to a gentle simmer.

Add the rice to the pan with the simmering liquid and stir constantly for 15 minutes, or until the rice is tender and almost all the liquid is absorbed. Stir in the egg, golden syrup and butter and mix well.

To serve, spoon the rice into serving dishes and pour the sherry over the top. Serve hot with stewed rhubarb or seasonal fruit on the side.

## crêpes with passionfruit and cottage cheese

100 g (3¹/₂ oz) unsalted butter
165 g (5³/₄ oz/1¹/₃ cups) plain (all-purpose)
    flour, sifted
2 eggs
2 egg yolks
2 tablespoons caster (superfine) sugar
500 ml (17 fl oz/2 cups) milk
1 tablespoon freshly squeezed lemon juice
vegetable oil, for frying
375 g (13 oz/1¹/₂ cups) cottage cheese
4 passionfruit, pulp only, plus extra, to garnish
caster (superfine) sugar, to taste

Serves 6

Passionfruit and cottage cheese rolled in a crêpe is the perfect 'at home' dessert.

To make the crêpes, heat the butter in a frying pan over medium heat and cook for 3 minutes, or until you can smell a nutty aroma and the butter starts to turn golden. Immediately remove from the pan, pour into a small heatproof jug and allow to cool.

Put the flour in a bowl and make a well in the centre. In a separate bowl, whisk together the eggs, egg yolks, sugar, milk, lemon juice and a pinch of salt. Pour the egg mixture into the well and gradually stir into the flour, then stir in the melted butter. Cover with plastic wrap and refrigerate for at least 2 hours.

Heat a little vegetable oil in a large frying pan over medium heat. Pour 2–3 tablespoons of batter into the frying pan at a time and tilt the pan to spread the mixture over the base — try to make a circle with a 20 cm (8 inch) diameter. Cook for 1 minute, or until the batter is set, and then gently flip and cook the other side. Gently remove the crêpe to a plate and keep warm in a low oven. Repeat with the remaining batter to make 12 crêpes in total.

Meanwhile, to make the filling, combine the cottage cheese and passionfruit pulp together in a bowl. Add the sugar, to taste, and stir to combine. Fill each warmed crêpe with about 2 tablespoons of filling and gently roll into a log. Garnish with the extra passionfruit pulp and serve.

# ti tina apple pie

## pastry

140 g (5 oz/1 heaped cup) plain (all-purpose) flour
30 g (1 oz/1/4 cup) icing (confectioners') sugar
80 g (2¾ oz) chilled unsalted butter, diced
1 teaspoon finely chopped lemon zest
1 egg yolk

## apple filling

8 granny smith apples, peeled, cored and sliced
200 g (7 oz/1 scant cup) raw (demerara) sugar
7 eggs yolks
80 g (2¾ oz/1/3 cup) caster (superfine) sugar
700 ml (24 fl oz) pouring (whipping) cream,
    plus extra, to serve
a pinch of ground cinnamon

Serves 8

To make the pastry, sift the flour and icing sugar into a large bowl. Using your fingertips, rub the butter into the flour until the mixture resembles coarse breadcrumbs. Add the lemon zest and egg yolk and stir with a flat-bladed knife. When the mixture starts to come together in small beads, gently gather together into a ball and knead the dough a couple of times on a lightly floured surface. Flatten into a disc, cover with plastic wrap and refrigerate for 30 minutes.

Lightly grease eight 10 x 2 cm (4 x ¾ inch) deep loose-based fluted flan (tartlet) tins, or one 25 x 6 cm (10 x 2½ inch) deep loose-based round flan (tart) tin.

Roll out the pastry between two sheets of baking paper to 2 mm (1/16 inch) thickness and cut to fit the base and side of the tin/s. Remove the top layer of baking paper and invert the pastry into the tin/s. Trim any excess pastry overhanging the edges. Lightly prick the base/s with a fork, then refrigerate for 30 minutes. Preheat the oven to 170ºC (325ºF/Gas 3).

Line the pastry shell/s with a sheet of crumpled baking paper and pour in some baking beads or uncooked rice. Bake for 15 minutes, remove the paper and beads and return to the oven for a further 5 minutes, or until lightly golden. Remove from the oven and set aside. Increase the oven temperature to 180ºC (350ºF/Gas 4).

To make the filling, put the apples and sugar in a frying pan over medium–high heat. Add a pinch of salt and cook for 30 minutes, or until the apples are caramelised and lightly golden around the edges. Remove from the heat and set aside until needed.

Whisk the egg yolks and caster sugar with electric beaters for 3 minutes, or until pale and fluffy. In a separate bowl mix the cream and cinnamon and stir to combine. Pour the egg mixture into the cream and stir. Gently fold through the apple mixture and combine well.

Pour the filling into the prepared pastry case/s and smooth over the top. Bake in the oven for 30 minutes, or until just set. Remove from the oven and allow to cool in the tin/s, before transferring to a wire rack to cool completely. Serve with cream, if desired.

Adults and kids will enjoy this take on a classic bread-and-butter pudding. I love this dessert when it is just baked, but it is also terrific cold the next day.

## banana croissant pudding

150 g (5$^1$/$_2$ oz) unsalted butter, softened
7 croissants, cut diagonally into 2 cm ($^3$/$_4$ inch) slices
4 ripe bananas, thickly sliced on the diagonal
60 g (2$^1$/$_4$ oz/$^1$/$_2$ cup) sultanas (golden raisins)
350 ml (12 fl oz) milk
350 ml (12 fl oz) pouring (whipping) cream
2 tablespoons dark rum (optional)
1 teaspoon ground nutmeg
1 vanilla bean, split lengthways, seeds scraped
6 egg yolks
175 g (6 oz/$^3$/$_4$ cup) caster (superfine) sugar, plus extra
vanilla ice cream or cream, to serve (optional)

Serves 6–8

Preheat the oven to 140°C (275°F/Gas 1). Grease a 20 x 30 cm (8 x 12 inch) deep baking dish and scatter a thin layer of sugar into the base of the dish.

Butter the croissant slices on both sides. Arrange one-third of the croissant slices in an even layer in the base of the dish. Arrange half the banana slices in an even layer over the top and sprinkle with half of the sultanas. Repeat this layering, finishing with the remaining crossaint slices on top.

Put the milk, cream, rum (if using) and nutmeg in a saucepan over medium heat. Add the vanilla bean and seeds to the pan and bring just to the boil. Reduce the heat and simmer for 2 minutes. Remove from the heat and then remove the vanilla bean. Set aside and allow to cool.

Meanwhile, whisk the egg yolks and sugar together with electric beaters for 3 minutes, or until light and fluffy.

Stir the milk into the eggs, mixing well, then pour the mixture over the croissants in the baking dish. Sit the dish in a large roasting tin and pour enough hot water into the tin to come halfway up the sides of the dish. Bake for 1 hour, or until cooked through; the top will spring back when pushed in.

This pudding is great served hot or cold, with ice cream or cream, and also tastes wonderful the day after baking.

Anything that grows at Possum Creek is more feral than organic — my produce has never had anything that resembles a chemical anywhere near it. You can really notice the true flavours of home-grown berries and this recipe is perfect to show them off.

## poached palm sugar berries

12 fresh lychees
4 tablespoons unsalted butter
300 g (10 1/2 oz/2 cups) grated palm sugar
    (jaggery)
600 g (1 lb 5 oz) fresh berries, such as blueberries,
    raspberries, blackberries or mulberries
a squeeze of lime or lemon juice
1 makrut (kaffir lime) leaf
1 vanilla bean, split lengthways
cream or ice cream, to serve (optional)

Serves 4

Peel the lychees. Cut a small slit in one side of each lychee and gently remove the stone.

Melt the butter and sugar in a frying pan over medium–high heat until the butter bubbles and the sugar liquifies. Add the berries and lychees and toss quickly to coat. Add 250 ml (9 fl oz/ 1 cup) water, the lime juice, makrut leaf, vanilla bean and a pinch of salt. Reduce the temperature and simmer for about 2 minutes, or until the berries are tender but not mushy. Poached palm sugar berries can be served warm or cold with cream or ice cream, if desired.

Goat's curd is a favourite ingredient of mine.
It tastes great with rhubarb and berries
and in this dish it really shines with the
wonderful flavours of cardamom apples.

# goat's curd bavarois with cardamom apples

### bavarois

4 large egg yolks
100 g ($3^1/_2$ oz/$^1/_2$ scant cup) caster (superfine) sugar
325 ml (11 fl oz) milk
2 tablespoons golden syrup (dark corn syrup)
$2^1/_2$ gelatine sheets (20 x 5 cm/8 x 2 inches)
400 g (14 oz/$3^1/_3$ cups) soft goat's curd

### cardamom apples

$^1/_2$ tablespoon cardamom seeds
3 tablespoons unsalted butter
4 granny smith apples, peeled, cored and sliced
4 heaped tablespoons soft brown sugar
4 tablespoons golden syrup (dark corn syrup)

Serves 8

To make the bavarois, whisk the egg yolks and sugar together in a heatproof bowl until pale and frothy.

Heat the milk in a saucepan over medium–high heat and bring almost to the boil. Remove from the heat and stir in the golden syrup.

Gradually stir the milk mixture into the egg mixture. Place the bowl over a saucepan of simmering water and stir for 20 minutes, or until the mixture thickens and coats the back of a spoon. Be careful not to overheat the mixture or it will curdle.

Meanwhile, soak the gelatine leaves in cold water for a few minutes, or until soft. Squeeze out any excess water and stir the gelatine into the hot custard until dissolved. Strain the custard, then set aside to cool.

Fold the goat's curd into the custard and combine well. Spoon into eight 100 ml ($3^1/_2$ fl oz) pudding moulds. Cover with plastic wrap and refrigerate for at least 4 hours, or until set.

Meanwhile, to make the cardamom apples, put the cardamom seeds and butter in a frying pan over low heat and cook for 3 minutes. Add the apples and sugar and cook for about 20 minutes, or until caramelised, stirring frequently. Add the golden syrup, 125 ml (4 fl oz/$^1/_2$ cup) water and a pinch of salt. Cook for 2 minutes further, or until the sauce thickens slightly.

To serve, briefly place the moulds upright in hot water to loosen slightly. Invert each mould onto a serving plate and spoon the warm cardamom apples and sauce over the top.

# chocolate mousse with honeycomb and espresso sauce

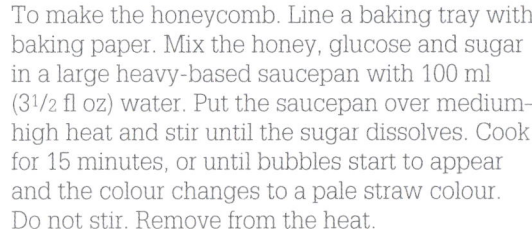

### honeycomb
40 g (1¹/₂ oz) honey
70 g (2¹/₂ oz) glucose syrup
200 g (7 oz) caster (superfine) sugar
1 teaspoon bicarbonate of soda (baking soda),
   sifted

### mousse
200 g (7 oz/1¹/₃ cups) chopped good-quality
   dark chocolate, such as couverture
   (see side note, page 219)
40 g (1¹/₂ oz) unsalted butter, chopped
4 eggs, separated
150 g (5¹/₂ oz/²/₃ heaped cup) sugar

### espresso sauce
250 ml (9 fl oz/1 cup) espresso coffee
100 g (3¹/₂ oz/¹/₂ cup) sugar
2 tablespoons kahlua

Serves 6

To make the honeycomb. Line a baking tray with baking paper. Mix the honey, glucose and sugar in a large heavy-based saucepan with 100 ml (3¹/₂ fl oz) water. Put the saucepan over medium–high heat and stir until the sugar dissolves. Cook for 15 minutes, or until bubbles start to appear and the colour changes to a pale straw colour. Do not stir. Remove from the heat.

Working quickly, stir in the bicarbonate of soda until it froths. Carefully pour the honeycomb mixture into the prepared baking tray and immediately place in the freezer. Freeze for 10–20 minutes, or until cooled. Break the honeycomb into large pieces and store in an airtight container in the freezer until needed.

To make the mousse, put the chocolate and butter in a small heatproof bowl over a small saucepan of simmering water, making sure the base of the bowl doesn't touch the water. Stir over low heat until melted, then remove from the heat.

Beat the egg yolks and sugar in a large bowl with electric beaters until thick, creamy and pale in colour. Gently fold through the chocolate mixture.

Whisk the egg whites until soft peaks form and fold carefully through the chocolate. Refrigerate for 3 hours, in the mixing bowl, or until set.

To make the espresso sauce, put the coffee, sugar and kahlua in a saucepan over medium–high heat and stir until the sugar dissolves. Bring to a boil, then reduce the heat to low and simmer for a further 15 minutes, or until slightly syrupy. Strain the sauce and allow to cool. Set aside until needed.

To serve, put a large spoonful of mousse in a martini glass, drizzle the espresso sauce over the top and add a shard of honeycomb.

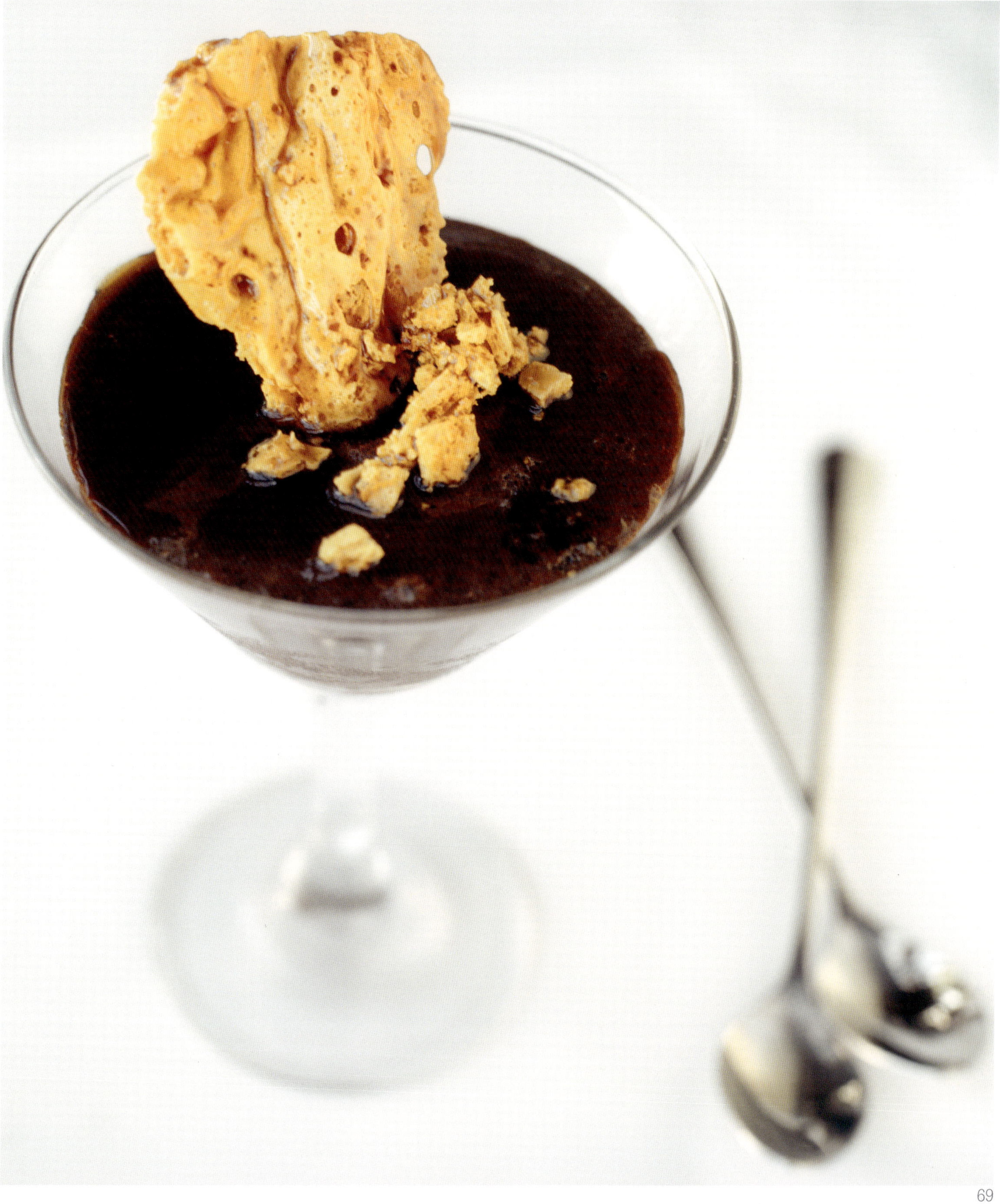

# dig that beet

**vegetarian food**

We all have to eat, but what we choose to eat is our decision. Fast food is everywhere; so is poor digestion. Perhaps it is the pace of life but often we eat for convenience with scant regard for health. Vegetables, although an excellent source of goodness, have an image problem in Australia. Perhaps memories of the overcooked vegetable mush we ate as children, have left an indelible stamp in our minds.

Too often, vegetarians go out for dinner only to find that many establishments will serve the barest and most basic possible options — hold the roast beef and only serve the vegies. Or they end up eating a salad and fries because the vegetarian options aren't cooked with any regard to health. Most of the vegetarians I know don't want to eat a heavy meal of pasta in a thick creamy sauce with only a scattering of fresh produce. Eating vegetables need not be like this, and at Fins it isn't.

Maybe you love seafood and juicy cuts of meat, or perhaps falafels and lentil patties are more your style. However, we all need great vegetarian dining options; they're not just for people who enjoy vegetarianism as a healthy lifestyle choice. There are thousands of different vegetables — all varying in texture, flavour, shape, complexity and colour. With a little imagination they can be transformed into flavoursome vegetarian dishes. One of the best things about cooking up a storm with vegetables is that it is relatively easy — try baking seasonal vegetables in preserved lemon, sumac and cinnamon and you're on your way to Morocco. Or how about deglazing vegetables with Champagne (or use a little of the wine you intend to enjoy with dinner) and adding a sprinkle of fresh thyme for extra zing? You can make a stock from shiitake mushrooms instead of beef, and if you want to go for the all-time simplest option, just barbecue vegetables for added 'wow'.

**I try to use my imagination when developing the vegetarian menu at Fins, not just because I like to offer interesting and well-balanced dining options to health-focused vegetarians, but because I am a fan of vegetables myself and I enjoy cooking with them. In this chapter I have included some of my favourites, from a Fijian creamy lentil soup with caramelised onion (see page 81), a hearty Brazilian bean soup (see page 82) and a Moroccan vegetable tagine (see page 93) to the more sophisticated Tallala green pea cakes with ginger spinach and corn (see page 78) and Japanese dumplings with tamarind ginger sauce and enoki tempura (see page 86). Desserts can also borrow their key ingredients from the vegetable kingdom. Surprise guests with avocado custard (see page 108) or a chocolate, macerated prune and beetroot brownie (see page 106).**

For many centuries, Chinese health practitioners, who draw no distinction between food and medicine, have prescribed vegetables and herbs in the battle against disease. In the West, including cabbage and carrots in the diet is widely believed to help combat cancer. Onions are good for the heart, and garlic is renowned for boosting immunity. On wintry nights, why not make those slow-cooked casseroles, curries, paellas and even soufflés vegetarian? Enjoy the feeling of eating something good for you, like pumpkin soufflé with a kick of spinach harissa (see page 90). Even better with a glass of pinot noir.

Perhaps my favourite vegetable of all is the colourful, voluptuous, versatile and glamorous beetroot. Beetroot adds excitement to salads and drama to soups. Its sweet, earthy flavour combines beautifully with the acid in wine. My favourite way to cook this sweet, earthy, sexy vegetable is with pinot noir in a risotto (see page 38). You can adapt this recipe and make it completely vegetarian by removing the anchovies and king prawns, using a vegetable stock and serving it with vegetables baked in lisbon paste (see page 226).

Rhubarb is gorgeous — a  mysterious plant with long, slender, ruby-coloured stalks, rich in vitamin C and dietary fibre. It is at its most enticing when used as a fruit, which is the best way to unleash its sophisticated tart flavour. Do not eat rhubarb raw, and ensure you strip it of its poisonous green leaves. There wouldn't be too many people who haven't enjoyed a rhubarb crumble. It's wonderful for breakfast with cereal or yoghurt or as a dessert with soft cheese, custard or cream. Add it to fruits such as apples, pears and berries. It is also great as a base for ice cream or jam and is a treat in a goat's curd tartlet (see page 102).

But what about the less obvious vegetable matter? Hawaiians love eating it, and in Japan it comprises 25 per cent of the local diet. Yet in Australia seaweed is just the stuff we're careful to step over while walking on the beach. It's high time we took our heads out of the sand and looked anew at seaweed's possibilities in the kitchen. Seaweeds, such as nori, arame and wakame, are high in iron and combine well with soy, sesame seeds and lemon juice. They are a natural in any stir-fry or salad and are delicious with rice.

# tallala green pea cakes with ginger spinach and corn

This dish was developed in the kitchen of Sri Lanka's Tallala Resort, where fresh produce from the garden forms the basis of every meal. In this most fertile and colourful country you can have anything you want for dinner as long as it's curried.

### green pea cakes

220 g (7¾ oz/1 cup) dried green split peas
1 small brown onion, roughly chopped
1 small green chilli, seeded and roughly chopped
1 teaspoon curry powder
2 garlic cloves, finely chopped
1.5 cm (⅝ inch) piece ginger, finely chopped
185 ml (6 fl oz/¾ cup) camellia tea oil (see note) or extra virgin olive oil, for frying

### ginger spinach and corn

2 tablespoons camellia tea oil or extra virgin olive oil
1 onion, thinly sliced
1–2 banana chillies, halved lengthways and finely sliced
3 large garlic cloves, finely sliced
1.5 cm (⅝ inch) piece ginger, finely chopped
1 teaspoon whole brown mustard seeds
¼ teaspoon cumin seeds
1 cm (½ inch) piece fresh turmeric, finely diced
250 g (9 oz/1 cup) tinned chopped tomatoes
½ teaspoon garam masala
280 g (10 oz) baby English spinach leaves
1 tablespoon butter
100 g (3½ oz/½ cup) cooked corn kernels
10 basil leaves, roughly torn
10 mint leaves, finely chopped
tamarind dressing (Basics, see page 231), to serve
½ pomegranate, seeds only, to garnish

Serves 10 as a canapé or 4–6 as an entrée

To make the pea cakes, cover the split peas with 1 litre (35 fl oz/4 cups) water and soak for 4 hours, or overnight. Drain and rinse the split peas and transfer them to a food processor. Add the onion, chilli, curry powder, garlic, ginger, ½ teaspoon salt and 60 ml (2 fl oz/¼ cup) water and blend until smooth. Set aside until needed.

To prepare the ginger spinach and corn, heat the oil in a large frying pan over medium–high heat. Add the onion and cook for 2 minutes, or until it has softened. Add the chilli, garlic, ginger, mustard seeds, cumin seeds and turmeric and cook for 2 minutes. Add the tomato and garam masala and cook for a further 2 minutes, then add the spinach and cook for 3 minutes, stirring until all the liquid has evaporated. Stir in the butter and corn, then lower the heat and simmer for 7 minutes. Add the basil and mint and stir through. Remove from the heat, cover and keep warm until ready to serve.

To cook the pea cakes, heat the oil in a large frying pan over medium heat. Working in batches, place 1 tablespoonful of the mixture into the pan at a time, pressing down lightly to flatten. Cook the cakes for 3 minutes each, or until brown on the bottom. Turn over and brown the other side for 2 minutes, or until golden and cooked through. Stack on a tray layered with paper towels and keep warm. You should make about 24 cakes in total.

To serve as an entrée, place a cake on each plate and layer 2 tablespoons of the ginger spinach and corn evenly over the top. Continue layering with another three cakes to create a four-cake stack on each plate. Drizzle the tamarind dressing around the stack and garnish with pomegranate seeds.

If serving as a canapé, place a spoonful of ginger spinach and corn on top of each cake and drizzle with a little dressing. Serve on platters.

note Camellia tea oil is a healthy, slightly sweet oil that smells of camellia tea. It is great with Asian foods and for cooking vegetables. It is available from most large supermarkets.

Fijians have a double-gene for friendliness. As a guest chef in Fiji you teach

## nd learn. This soup is one that I learnt.

# fijian creamy lentil soup with caramelised onion

375 g (13 oz/1½ cups) red lentils
1 litre (35 fl oz/4 cups) vegetable stock or water
½ teaspoon ground turmeric
2.5 cm (1 inch) piece ginger, peeled and
    chopped
2 tomatoes, chopped
250 ml (9 fl oz/1 cup) milk
60 g (2¼ oz) unsalted butter
1 brown onion, diced
1 teaspoon cumin seeds
small handful coriander (cilantro) leaves,
    finely chopped (optional)

Serves 6

Pick over the lentils, removing any stones or
discoloured ones. Rinse thoroughly and place
in a deep stainless-steel or other non-metallic
saucepan with the vegetable stock or water,
turmeric, ginger and tomato. Bring to the boil
over medium–high heat, then reduce the heat and
simmer, uncovered, for 25 minutes, or until the
lentils are soft.

Remove from the heat and allow to cool slightly
before transferring to a food processor and
blending until smooth. Return the puréed lentils
to the warm pan, stir in the milk and 1 teaspoon
sea salt and simmer gently over low heat until
ready to serve.

Meanwhile, melt the butter in a frying pan over
high heat. Add the onion and cumin seeds and
cook, stirring occasionally, for 8 minutes, or until
the onions are brown and caramelised.

To serve, ladle the soup into warm bowls and
sprinkle generously with cracked black pepper,
to taste. Scatter the caramelised onion and
coriander over the soup and serve immediately.

It is usually 'peasant food', cooked with local produce, leftovers and love, that interests me. This soup is an exotic mix of native Indian, African and Portuguese cooking.

## brazilian bean soup

100 g (3½ oz/½ cup) white beans, such as cannellini or navy beans
100 g (3½ oz/½ cup) dried black beans
100 g (3½ oz/½ cup) dried red kidney beans
200 ml (7 fl oz) extra virgin olive oil
4 brown onions, finely sliced
6 garlic cloves, crushed
6 coriander (cilantro) roots, finely sliced
2 small carrots, finely sliced
2 leeks, sliced into 1 cm (½ inch) rounds
300 g (10½ oz/1¼ cups) tinned chopped tomatoes
2 tablespoons ground cumin
½ tablespoon smoked paprika
125 ml (4 fl oz/½ cup) white wine
½ teaspoon saffron threads, steeped in 150 ml (5 fl oz) hot water for 20 minutes
4 litres (140 fl oz/16 cups) vegetable stock
flat-leaf (Italian) parsley, chopped, to serve

Serves 8

Place the beans in a non-metallic bowl, cover with water and leave to soak for at least 8 hours or preferably overnight.

Discard any beans that float, then rinse thoroughly. Put the beans in a saucepan, cover with fresh water and bring to the boil over high heat, then reduce the heat and simmer for 45 minutes, or until soft. Make sure you only cook at a simmer so the beans retain their shape and don't start breaking up. Drain well.

In a separate stockpot or very large saucepan, heat the olive oil over medium heat. Add the onion, garlic, coriander root, carrot and leek. Cook for 10 minutes, or until the onion is lightly golden. Add the tomato, cumin and smoked paprika and cook for a further 2 minutes, or until fragrant. Add the beans and wine and stir. Bring to the boil and cook for 2 minutes. Add the saffron threads and stock, reduce the heat and simmer for 30 minutes for the flavours to meld. Season with sea salt and cracked black pepper, to taste.

Serve in warm bowls and scatter with parsley, to garnish.

## japanese dumplings with tamarind ginger sauce and enoki tempura

### tamarind ginger sauce

60 ml (2 fl oz/¼ cup) camellia tea oil (see note
    on page 82) or extra virgin olive oil
3 garlic cloves, finely chopped
5 cm (2 inch) piece ginger, finely sliced
1 large onion, finely sliced
60 ml (2 fl oz/¼ cup) light soy sauce
60 ml (2 fl oz/¼ cup) kecap manis
70 ml (2¼ fl oz) tamarind water (Basics, see
    page 231)
½ makrut (kaffir lime) leaf, finely sliced
500 g (1 lb 2 oz/2 cups) tinned chopped tomatoes

### dumplings

2 tablespoons olive oil
½ brown onion, finely chopped
2 garlic cloves, finely chopped
1.5 cm (⅝ inch) piece ginger, finely chopped
325 g (11½ oz) tempeh, finely diced
70 g (2½ oz) silken tofu, finely diced
60 g (2¼ oz/⅓ cup) cooked jasmine rice
3 tablespoons shaoxing rice wine
2 tablespoons kecap manis
1 tablespoon soy sauce
1 teaspoon truffle oil
30 g (1 oz/½ cup) panko (Japanese breadcrumbs)
24 round gow gee wrappers
100 g (3½ oz) enoki mushrooms
90 g (3¼ oz/½ cup) rice flour
250 ml (9 fl oz/1 cup) tempura batter (Basics,
    see page 231)
vegetable oil, for deep-frying
8 snow peas (mangetout), cut on the diagonal
    into 3 cm (1¼ inch) pieces
seaweed salad (Basics, see page 229), to serve
parsley oil (Basics, see page 227), to garnish
    (optional)

Serves 8

This is probably the most ordered vegetarian dish on the Fins menu.
Dumplings are comforting but with a tamarind ginger sauce and
Japanese embellishments they become quite special!

To make the tamarind ginger sauce, heat the oil in a saucepan over medium–high heat and add the garlic, ginger and onion. Cook for 5 minutes, or until lightly golden. Add the soy sauce, kecap manis and tamarind water and bring to the boil. Add the makrut leaf and simmer for 10 minutes, or until the liquid is reduced by half. Add the tomatoes and 200 ml (7 fl oz) water and gently simmer for 10 minutes.

Remove from the heat and allow to cool slightly, before transferring to a food processor and blending until smooth. Pass through a sieve and return to a clean saucepan. Gently reheat when ready to serve.

To make the dumplings, heat the oil in a large frying pan over medium–high heat. Add the onion, garlic and ginger and cook for 5 minutes, or until golden. Add the tempeh, tofu and cooked rice and cook for a further 3 minutes to heat through, stirring to combine. Add the rice wine, kecap manis, soy sauce and truffle oil. Bring to the boil and cook until almost all of the liquid has evaporated. Remove from the heat and allow to cool slightly. Transfer to a food processor, add the breadcrumbs and blend until smooth.

Place a gow gee wrapper in the palm of your hand. Put a tablespoon of the tempeh mixture in the centre. Lightly brush the edge with water and fold in half to enclose the filling, pinching to seal. Join opposite ends together to form a dumpling. Continue until all the filling has been used – you should make 24 dumplings in total.

Place the dumplings on a tray and cover with plastic wrap; they can be stored in the refrigerator for up to 3 days. Alternatively, you can place them in a sealed container and freeze for up to 2 weeks before cooking.

Fill a deep-fryer or large heavy-based saucepan one-third full of oil and heat to 180°C (350°F). Trim 1 cm (½ inch) from the root ends of the enoki mushrooms, leaving the bunch intact. Divide the enoki into eight small even-sized bunches. Dust the enoki in rice flour, then dip into the batter. Deep-fry the enoki, for about 2 minutes, or until lightly golden. Drain on paper towels and season with sea salt.

Meanwhile, blanch the snow peas briefly in a saucepan of boiling water, then drain well. Keep warm until ready to serve.

Lower the dumplings into a large saucepan of simmering water for 3–4 minutes, (you may need to do this in batches), until warmed through. Remove with a slotted spoon and drain on a clean tea towel (dish towel).

To serve, place about 3 tablespoons of the tamarind ginger sauce on each plate. Arrange three dumplings over the sauce and top with the seaweed salad. Sit the enoki on top and garnish with snow peas and parsley oil, if desired.

# portuguese vegetables with polenta chips

### polenta chips

70 g (2¹/2 oz) butter
150 g (5¹/2 oz/1 cup) fine instant polenta
200 g (7 oz/2 cups) grated parmesan cheese
vegetable oil, for deep-frying

1 large brown onion, cut into 8 wedges
4 small garlic cloves, peeled
2 small zucchini, cut into quarters lengthways
2 small carrots, peeled and cut into quarters
    lengthways
2 small Japanese eggplants (aubergines), cut into
    quarters lengthways
1 red capsicum (pepper), seeded and membrane
    removed, cut into 1 cm (¹/2 inch) strips
12 green beans, trimmed
250 ml (9 fl oz/1 cup) extra virgin olive oil
¹/2 teaspoon smoked paprika
2 fresh bay leaves
290 ml (10 fl oz) tomato sauce (Basics, see
    page 231), warmed, to serve

Serves 4

Preheat the oven to 190°C (375°F/Gas 5).

To make the polenta chips, put 750 ml (26 fl oz/ 3 cups) water in a saucepan over high heat and bring to the boil. Add the butter and a pinch of sea salt, then add the polenta and stir continuously for 20 minutes, or until cooked. Remove from the heat and stir in the parmesan cheese to combine. Pour into a 25 x 10 x 3 cm (10 x 4 x 1¼ inch) baking tray and spread out evenly to 1.5 cm (⅝ inch) thickness. Refrigerate for 1 hour, or until set.

To make the vegetables, place the onions, garlic, zucchini, carrot, eggplant, capsicum and beans in a large baking dish. Combine the olive oil, paprika, bay leaves and 1 tablespoon sea salt and toss to coat the vegetables. Cook in the oven for 20 minutes, or until tender and lightly golden. Alternatively, you can chargrill them on a barbecue for 5 minutes. Keep warm until ready to serve.

Cut the polenta into 10 cm (4 inch) long chips. Fill a deep-fryer or large heavy-based saucepan one-third full of oil and heat to 180°C (350°F). Deep-fry the polenta chips, in batches if necessary, for about 3 minutes each, or until crisp and golden. Drain on paper towels.

To serve, place about 3 tablespoons warm tomato sauce on each plate and stack the polenta chips and vegetables on top.

## pumpkin soufflés with spinach harissa

1 tablespoon butter
30 g (1 oz/¼ cup) semolina
350 g (12 oz) jap or kent pumpkin (winter squash),
    seeded, skinned and diced
80 ml (2½ fl oz/⅓ cup) olive oil
½ preserved lemon, zest only, rinsed and finely
    chopped (Basics, see page 227)
1 handful coriander (cilantro) leaves, chopped
40 g (1½ oz) butter
50 g (1¾ oz/⅓ cup) plain (all-purpose) flour
350 ml (12 fl oz) milk, warmed
3 eggs, separated
1 orange sweet potato, peeled
vegetable oil, for deep-frying
200 g (7 oz/4 cups) baby English spinach leaves
1 tablespoon harissa (Basics, see page 224)
baby watercress, to garnish

Serves 4

Preheat the oven to 220°C (425°F/Gas 7). Grease four 200 ml (7 fl oz) ramekins with the butter and dust with the semolina.

To make the soufflés, toss 150 g (5½ oz) diced pumpkin in 3 tablespoons of the olive oil and place on a baking tray. Roast in the oven for 15–20 minutes, or until soft and lightly golden.

Meanwhile, put the remaining pumpkin in a double-boiler and steam for 10 minutes, or until tender. Remove from the heat, mash the pumpkin and then push through a fine sieve. Add the preserved lemon and coriander and stir to combine. Add the diced roast pumpkin to the mashed pumpkin mixture and keep warm.

Melt the butter in a saucepan over low heat and add the flour, stirring continuously until smooth. Gradually stir through the warm milk to make a thick béchamel sauce. Cook the sauce, stirring continuously, for 10–15 minutes, or until very thick. Season with sea salt and cracked black pepper, to taste. Remove from the heat.

Whisk the egg whites and a pinch of salt with an electric mixer until stiff peaks form. Mix the egg yolks into the béchamel, then gently fold through the pumpkin mixture. Fold in the egg whites. Spoon the mixture into the ramekins and

place in a deep baking dish. Pour enough hot water into the dish to sit one-third of the way up the side of the ramekins. Bake the soufflés for 2 minutes and then lower the oven temperature to 170°C (325°F/Gas 3). Continue cooking for a further 15–20 minutes, or until the soufflés have risen and are golden.

While the soufflés are cooking, slice the sweet potato into long strips with a vegetable peeler. Fill a deep-fryer or large heavy-based saucepan one-third full of vegetable oil and heat to 180°C (350°F). Deep-fry the sweet potato strips for 2 minutes, or until crisp and golden. Drain on paper towels.

Meanwhile, heat the remaining olive oil in a frying pan over medium heat and add the spinach, tossing quickly until wilted. Add the harissa and stir through to combine, then remove from the heat. Season with sea salt, to taste.

Arrange the spinach on four serving plates — the harissa will drizzle out onto the plate. Remove the soufflés from the oven and allow to cool slightly. Run a knife around the inside rim of the ramekins and gently turn the soufflés out over the spinach. Serve with the sweet potato chips on top and garnish with baby watercress.

# moroccan vegetable tagine

### fennel purée
50 g (1¾ oz) butter
1 brown onion, sliced
1 garlic clove
3 fennel bulbs, finely sliced
1 tablespoon freshly squeezed lemon juice

### sweet potato base
150 ml (5 fl oz) extra virgin olive oil or
    Moroccan argan oil (see note)
2 brown onions, finely chopped
2 garlic cloves, finely chopped
1 fresh bay leaf
500 g (1 lb 2 oz) sweet potato, diced
400 g (14 oz/2 cups) cooked chickpeas
250 g (9 oz/1 cup) tinned chopped tomatoes
1 preserved lemon, zest only, rinsed and finely
    sliced (Basics, see page 227)
1 tablespoon sumac
3 cinnamon sticks
350 ml (12 fl oz) white wine
200 g (7 oz/1¼ cups) chopped fresh pitted dates

185 ml (6 fl oz/¾ cup) olive oil
1 brown onion, finely chopped
1 garlic clove, finely chopped
1 red capsicum (pepper), seeded, membrane
    removed and cut into 2 cm (¾ inch) pieces
1 large eggplant (aubergine), chopped into
    2 cm (¾ inch) pieces
2 large field mushrooms, chopped
1 zucchini (courgette), chopped
1 teaspoon smoked paprika
100 ml (3½ fl oz) white wine

Serves 6

To make the fennel purée, melt the butter in a saucepan over medium heat. Add the onion, garlic and fennel, and cook for 20 minutes, or until the fennel is soft. Remove from the heat and allow to cool slightly, before transferring to a food processor. Add the lemon juice, season with sea salt and cracked black pepper and blend until smooth. Return to a clean saucepan and gently reheat before serving.

To make the sweet potato base, heat the olive oil in a large saucepan over high heat. Add the onion, garlic and bay leaf and cook for 5 minutes, or until lightly golden. Add the sweet potato, chickpeas, tomatoes, preserved lemon, sumac and cinnamon and stir to combine. Add the wine, bring to the boil, then reduce the heat and simmer for about 3 minutes, stirring occasionally. Add the dates and cook for a further 5 minutes, or until the sweet potato is tender. Remove from the heat, cover and keep warm until ready to serve.

Meanwhile, heat the olive oil in a saucepan over high heat. Add the onion, garlic and capsicum and cook for 10 minutes, or until golden and soft. Add the eggplant, mushroom, zucchini, paprika and wine and bring to the boil. Reduce the heat, cover and simmer for 10 minutes, or until the vegetables are tender.

To serve, place the sweet potato mixture in the bottom of a tagine to form a base. Arrange the vegetables over the top and drizzle with the fennel purée.

note Argan oil is produced from the fruits of the argan tree which is endemic to Morocco. It has a walnut-type flavour and tastes great with couscous and salads. It is available from Middle Eastern food stores or specialist delicatessens.

# pumpkin tartlets with tomato, goat's cheese and caramelised onion

## pastry
175 g (6 oz/1$^1$/$_2$ cups) plain (all-purpose) flour
125 g (4$^1$/$_2$ oz) chilled butter, diced
1 egg
$^1$/$_2$ tablespoon finely chopped parsley

## caramelised onion
2 tablespoons vegetable oil
2 brown onions, finely sliced
55 g (2 oz/$^1$/$_4$ cup) sugar
3 tablespoons balsamic vinegar

## pumpkin filling
100 g (3$^1$/$_2$ oz) butter
1 onion, finely sliced
2 garlic cloves, finely chopped
300 g (10$^1$/$_2$ oz) jap or kent pumpkin (winter
    squash), cut into 2 cm ($^3$/$_4$ inch) pieces
$^1$/$_2$ teaspoon ground cinnamon
$^1$/$_2$ teaspoon ground nutmeg
125 ml (4 fl oz/$^1$/$_2$ cup) white wine
125 g (4$^1$/$_2$ oz/$^1$/$_2$ cup) tomato sauce (Basics, see
    page 231), to serve
60 g (2$^1$/$_4$ oz/$^1$/$_2$ cup) crumbled goat's curd, to
    serve

Makes 24 tartlets

To make the pastry, preheat the oven to 160°C (315°F/Gas 2–3). Lightly grease twenty-four 5 cm (2 inch) round and 1 cm (½ inch) deep fluted tartlet tins.

Sift the flour into a large bowl. Using your fingertips, rub the butter into the flour until the mixture resembles coarse breadcrumbs. Add the egg and parsley and stir with a flat-bladed knife. When the mixture starts to come together in small beads, gently gather together into a ball and knead the dough a couple of times on a lightly floured surface. Flatten into a disc, cover with plastic wrap and refrigerate for 30 minutes.

Roll out the pastry between two sheets of baking paper to 5 mm ($^1$/$_4$ inch) thickness. Cut into twenty-four discs with a 7 cm (2$^3$/$_4$ inch) diameter to fit the base and side of each tartlet. Lightly prick the bases with a fork. Refrigerate for 30 minutes.

Line the pastry shells with squares of lightly crumpled baking paper and pour in some baking beads or uncooked rice. Bake for 7–8 minutes. Remove the paper and rice or beads and bake for a further 5 minutes, or until lightly golden. Remove from the oven and set aside.

To make the caramelised onion, heat the oil in a saucepan over medium heat and sauté the onion for 15 minutes, or until softened. Add the sugar and vinegar, reduce the heat and simmer for a further 45 minutes, or until the liquid has been absorbed and the onions are caramelised. Set aside.

Meanwhile, make the pumpkin filling. Heat the butter in a saucepan over medium heat and add the onion and garlic. Cook for 5 minutes, or until the onion has softened. Add the pumpkin, cinnamon and nutmeg and season with sea salt and cracked black pepper. Add 100 ml (3$^1$/$_2$ fl oz) water and simmer for 15–20 minutes, or until the pumpkin is soft. Remove from the heat and allow to cool slightly, before transferring to a food processor and blending until smooth. Adjust the seasoning, to taste. Set aside.

Fill each tartlet with the pumpkin mixture, then add a teaspoon each of caramelised onion and tomato sauce. Spoon a small amount of goat's curd over each.

# vegetable paella

1 teaspoon saffron threads
1 large red capsicum (pepper)
3 tablespoons olive oil
2 large brown onions, sliced
3 garlic cloves, finely sliced
2 fresh bay leaves
1 teaspoon smoked paprika
500 g (1 lb 2 oz/2¾ cups) Calaspara rice
    (see note) or paella rice
2 tablespoons lisbon paste (Basics, see page 226)
250 ml (9 fl oz/1 cup) white wine
1 large zucchini (courgette), cut into 5 mm
    (¼ inch) thick batons
24 green beans, trimmed
6 baby (pattypan) squash, cut into 5 mm (¼ inch)
    rounds
1 large eggplant (aubergine), cut lengthways
    into 5 mm (¼ inch) slices
1 large corn cob, kernels removed
12 asparagus spears, trimmed of woody ends
250 ml (9 fl oz/1 cup) mediterranean marinade
    (Basics, see page 226)
12 pitted kalamata olives, cut in half
lemon slices, to garnish
1 handful parsley leaves, chopped, to garnish

Serves 6

## This is a wonderful take on a traditional Spanish dish — with delicious chargrilled vegetables and saffron rice in a tasty Mediterranean marinade.

Dissolve the saffron threads in 2 litres (70 fl oz/ 8 cups) hot water and stand for 20 minutes for the saffron to infuse. Preheat the grill (broiler) to high. Cut the capsicum in half and remove the membrane and seeds. Place the capsicum, skin side up, under the grill until the skin blackens and blisters. Cool in a plastic bag, then peel the skin. Discard the seeds and membrane and slice lengthways into 5 mm (¼ inch) strips. Set aside.

Heat the olive oil in a saucepan over medium– high heat and add the onion, garlic, bay leaves and paprika and cook for 5 minutes, or until the onion has softened. Add the rice and stir to coat in the oil. Stir in the lisbon paste and cook for a further 3 minutes, then add the wine and stir for a few minutes, or until absorbed in the rice.

Add the saffron stock to the pan and bring to the boil. Reduce the heat, cover with a tight-fitting lid and cook for 20 minutes, or until the rice is just tender. Remove from the heat and spread the rice out on a large tray to cool (this will stop the cooking process). Cover to keep warm and set aside until needed.

Meanwhile, prepare the vegetables. Coat all the vegetables with the marinade. Place on a barbecue chargrill plate or ridged chargrill pan and cook over medium–high heat for 5 minutes, or until cooked through. Arrange the vegetables over the rice. Garnish with the lemon slices, chopped parsley and kalamata olives, to serve.

note Calaspara rice is from Valencia in Spain and is typically used for making paella. You can substitute jasmine rice or other short-grain rice if it is unavailable.

# Japanese vegetarian tasting plate

### tofu sandwich

900 g (2 lb) silken tofu, cut into six equal slices, then halved
1 nori (seaweed) sheet, cut into tiny strips
2 tablespoons mirin
2 tablespoons sake
2 tablespoons white miso paste
rice flour, for dusting

### tempura vegetables

1 carrot, peeled
12 green beans, trimmed
100 g (3¹/₂ oz) enoki mushrooms, roots trimmed
12 snow peas (mangetout), trimmed
1 red capsicum (pepper), seeded and membrane removed
rice flour, for dusting
500 ml (17 fl oz/2 cups) tempura batter (Basics, see page 231)
vegetable oil, for deep-frying
yuzu mayonnaise (Basics, see page 232), to serve

Serves 6

To make the tofu sandwiches, lay six tofu slices on a tray covered with a tea towel (dish towel). Sprinkle one teaspoon of nori strips on each tofu slice. Place the remaining six tofu halves on top to create sandwiches. Cover with another tea towel and place a baking sheet topped with a dinner plate on top to compress the tofu. Refrigerate for at least 3 hours or overnight.

Put the mirin and sake in a saucepan over high heat and cook for 2 minutes to burn off the alcohol. Add the miso and cook over low heat for 1 minute. Remove from the heat and set aside.

To make the tempura vegetables, cut the carrot into 1 cm (¹/₂ inch) rounds. Plunge the beans into a saucepan of boiling water for 3 minutes, to blanch, then refresh in a bowl of iced water. Cut the enoki mushrooms at the stem into six equal bunches. Cut the capsicum into 1 cm (¹/₂ inch) wide strips.

Fill a deep-fryer or large heavy-based saucepan one-third full of oil and heat to 180°C (350°F). Remove the weights from the tofu and pat dry any damp areas with a dry tea towel. Dust the tofu sandwiches in rice flour. Using a slotted spoon, deep-fry the tofu sandwiches, one at a time, for 2 minutes each, or until golden. Drain on paper towels.

Dust all of the cut vegetables in rice flour to coat, then dip in the tempura batter. Deep-fry the vegetables, in batches, for 3 minutes each, or until crisp and golden. Drain on paper towels and season with sea salt.

Put 1 tablespoon of miso sauce mixture on the top of each tofu sandwich and place under a preheated grill (broiler) for 2 minutes, or until golden.

Arrange the tempura vegetables and tofu sandwiches on a large serving platter and serve with the yuzu mayonnaise.

Wakaya Club in Fiji is an ultra-exclusive resort frequented by the world's celebrities. During my stay, as a guest chef, I learnt everything there is to know about coconuts, and prepared this dish many times.

## wakaya club fresh coconut vanilla ice cream

2 young coconuts, flesh removed and juice
    reserved (see note)
1/2 vanilla bean, split lengthways, seeds scraped
2 tablespoons maple syrup
1 tablespoon soft brown sugar
fresh mangoes, to serve

Serves 6

Put the coconut flesh, vanilla seeds, maple syrup and sugar into a food processor and process, adding the coconut juice a little at a time until the mixture is quite smooth (you may not need to use all the juice). Transfer to an ice-cream machine and freeze according to the manufacturer's instructions. Alternatively, place in a container and freeze for at least 4 hours, whisking the mixture every 15 minutes to create a creamier consistency.

Serve the Wakaya ice cream with fresh mango cheeks or slices. You can also serve the cream, unfrozen, if desired.

note The juice is what is inside the cavity when you crack the coconut open, while the cream and milk come from pressing the grated coconut (see side panel).

### coconut cream and milk

The process of extracting the coconut cream and milk from the coconut may seem labour-intensive but is well worth the effort. The best coconut cream is made from old, dry coconuts. It is essential to peel the brown skin so that the cream looks clean and pure.

To make coconut cream, grate the coconut flesh with a hand grater or food processor. Measure the flesh and add half the measured amount in water. Stir or blend at high speed to thoroughly combine. Place the mixture inside a square of muslin (cheesecloth) and squeeze the liquid into a bowl. Allow to stand for 20 minutes, for the cream to rise to the top, and then skim it off with a spoon. The object is to use as little water as possible to create a wet paste, which will make it easier to squeeze the cream out.

To make coconut milk you repeat this process using the squeezed flesh and another 250 ml (9 fl oz/1 cup) water, thus creating a thinner, less concentrated version of the cream.

Both coconut cream and milk can be frozen and stored for later use. Coconut milk will solidify in the refrigerator, so place it on a work surface until it reaches room temperature and whisk thoroughly before adding to any recipe.

# rhubarb and goat's curd tartlets

### pastry
140 g (5 oz/1 heaped cup) plain (all-purpose) flour
30 g (1 oz/$^1$/$_4$ cup) icing (confectioners') sugar
75 g (2$^3$/$_4$ oz) chilled unsalted butter, cubed
1 teaspoon finely chopped lemon zest
1 egg yolk

### filling
35 g (1$^1$/$_4$ oz/$^1$/$_4$ cup) goat's curd
1$^1$/$_2$ tablespoons golden syrup (1 tablespoon dark
    corn syrup with $^1$/$_2$ tablespoon honey)
1$^1$/$_2$ tablespoons icing (confectioners') sugar
70 g (2$^1$/$_2$ oz/$^1$/$_3$ cup) thick (double/heavy) cream

### rhubarb compote
180 g (6$^1$/$_2$ oz/$^3$/$_4$ heaped cup) sugar
1$^1$/$_2$ tablespoons freshly squeezed lemon juice
500 g (1 lb 2 oz/4 cups) chopped rhubarb
    (cut into 2 cm/$^3$/$_4$ inch) lengths

Serves 5

Sift the flour and icing sugar into a bowl. Lightly rub the butter into the flour with your fingertips until the mixture resembles breadcrumbs. Add the lemon zest and egg yolk and stir with a flat-bladed knife. When the mixture starts to come together in small beads, gently gather together into a ball and knead the dough a couple of times on a lightly floured surface. Flatten into a disc, cover with plastic wrap and refrigerate for 30 minutes.

Preheat the oven to 180°C (350°F/Gas 4). Lightly grease five 10 cm (4 inch) wide and 2 cm ($^3$/$_4$ inch) deep, round loose-based tartlet tins.

Roll out the pastry between two sheets of baking paper to 5 mm ($^1$/$_4$ inch) thick. Lift off the top layer of baking paper. Cut into 15 cm (6 inch) rounds, just slightly bigger than the tartlet tins. Carefully place a round into each tin and trim any excess pastry, removing the remaining baking paper. Lightly prick the bases with a fork, then refrigerate for 30 minutes.

Line the pastry shells with a small sheet of crumpled baking paper and pour in some baking beads or uncooked rice. Bake for 15 minutes, remove the paper and beads and return the pastry cases to the oven for a further 5 minutes, or until golden. Remove from the oven and cool.

To make the filling, fold the goat's curd, golden syrup and icing sugar together until combined. Add the cream and fold through. Cover with plastic wrap and refrigerate for at least 30 minutes.

To make the rhubarb compote, put the sugar and lemon juice with 100 ml (3$^1$/$_2$ fl oz) water in a small saucepan over medium–high heat. Stir until the sugar dissolves. Add the rhubarb and a pinch of salt. Increase the heat and bring to a boil. Cook for 2 minutes, or until the rhubarb is tender, then remove from the heat. Allow to cool, then strain into a bowl, reserving some of the syrup to use as a garnish.

Spoon the filling into the pastry cases and top with the rhubarb pieces. To serve, drizzle a little of the rhubarb syrup over the top of each tart.

### rhubarb

Rhubarb tastes great served with breakfast cereals, yoghurt, vanilla ice cream, cream and fruit salad. You can use it in crumbles and add it to smoothies. You can even make a simple mousse by stirring cooked rhubarb through some thick (double/heavy) cream and serving in a tall glass. The best way to cook a bunch of rhubarb is to trim the ends of the stalks and then cut the rest into 4 cm (1 1/2 inch) lengths, which can then be used in a variety of ways. Place in a heavy-based stainless-steel saucepan with a tight-fitting lid over medium heat. Add 235 g (8 1/2 oz/ 1 cup) caster (superfine) sugar, 1 tablespoon water and 1 lemon cut into quarters. Stir, cover and cook for 10 minutes, or until the rhubarb is soft, like a purée. Before purchasing, check that the rhubarb stalks are strong, crisp and fresh-looking. Rhubarb can also react with some cookware, so avoid using aluminium pans.

This chocolate gelato is simple to prepare — a no-cook ice cream that tastes great served with Frangelico.

## chocolate gelato

1/2 vanilla bean, split lengthways, seeds scraped
55 g (2 oz/1/4 cup) caster (superfine) sugar
375 ml (13 fl oz/1 1/2 cups) oat, almond or
    cow's milk
250 ml (9 fl oz/1 cup) coconut milk (see page 101
    for extraction method)
325 g (11 1/2 oz/1 1/2 cups) chopped coconut flesh
90 g (3 1/4 oz/1/4 cup) golden syrup (dark corn
    syrup)
30 g (1 oz/1/4 cup) unsweetened cocoa powder
2 tablespoons vegetable oil

Makes 1 litre (35 fl oz/4 cups)

Whisk the vanilla seeds and sugar together to combine well.

Put the vanilla sugar, milk, coconut milk, coconut flesh, golden syrup, cocoa powder and vegetable oil into a food processor and blend until smooth.

Transfer the mixture to an ice-cream machine to churn and freeze according to the manufacturer's instructions. Alternatively, transfer to a shallow tray and freeze, whisking every 15 minutes until frozen (this will give the gelato a creamier texture).

## chocolate, macerated prune & beetroot brownie

125 g (4¹/2 oz) unsalted butter
280 g (10 oz/2 cups) chopped good-quality dark
    chocolate, such as couverture (see note,
    page 219)
250 g (9 oz/1¹/3 cups) soft brown sugar
3 large eggs
175 g (6 oz/1¹/2 cups) plain (all-purpose) flour,
    sifted
125 g (4¹/2 oz/1 cup) unsweetened cocoa powder,
    sifted
150 g (5¹/2 oz/1 cup) freshly grated raw beetroot
    (beet)
150 g (5¹/2 oz/²/3 cup) pitted prunes, finely chopped
    and soaked overnight in cream sherry

Serves 8–10

Preheat the oven to 180°C (350°F/Gas 4). Lightly
grease a 20 x 30 x 3 cm (8 x 12 x 1¹/4 inch)
rectangular slice tin and line the base and sides
with baking paper.

Melt the butter and chocolate in a heatproof bowl
over a saucepan of simmering water. Remove from
the heat and allow to cool slightly.

Put the sugar and eggs in a bowl and whisk to
combine. Add the melted chocolate and stir
thoroughly. Add the flour, cocoa and a pinch of salt
to the mixture and stir to combine, then gently fold
through the grated beetroot and the prunes.

Pour the mixture into the prepared tin and bake
for 35 minutes, or until the top is dry to the touch
all over. Remove from the oven and allow to cool
in the tin for 10 minutes, before turning out onto a
wire rack to cool completely. Cut into squares and
serve. I like to serve it with cream garnished with
a toffee shard.

## beetroot

Nutritionally, beetroot has no fat, few kilojoules and it is rich in fibre with valuable antioxidants and B-group vitamins. There is no need to waste any part of the beetroot. First, remove the leaves, which are edible: wash them, then blanch them quickly in lightly salted boiling water. Alternatively, you can stir-fry the leaves in a little olive oil and add them to salads, casseroles, soups or pasta.

To cook the beetroot, trim the tops, leaving 2 cm (¾ inch) of stalk attached. This stops the beetroot from 'bleeding'. Wash the beetroot well to remove all soil and cover with lightly salted water. Boil for 30 to 60 minutes or until the beetroot is cooked — you should be able to easily insert a fine skewer.

Beetroots are most flavoursome when baked. To do this, wrap them in foil and cook them at 180°C (350°F/Gas 4) for 90 minutes or until tender. Small beets are great for pickling. Boil them, then preserve them in balsamic or raspberry vinegar with a little orange rind and dill tips. Refrigerate until you get hungry.

Fresh beetroot should be firm, with smooth skin and no cracks or splits, and the leaves should be intact. They can be stored in the refrigerator for 10 days.

# avocado custard

2 ripe avocados, peeled, stones removed
    and flesh cut into slices
80 g (2³/₄ oz/¹/₃ cup) caster (superfine) sugar
a pinch of ground cinnamon
a pinch of ground ginger
1 egg
1 egg yolk
¹/₂ teaspoon natural vanilla extract
250 ml (9 fl oz/1 cup) milk
1 tablespoon port wine
ice cream or cream, to serve

Serves 4

Preheat the oven to 150°C (300°F/Gas 2).

Put the avocados, sugar, cinnamon, ginger, egg
and egg yolk, vanilla, milk and port wine into a
food processor and blend until smooth. Strain the
liquid and pour into four 125 ml (4 fl oz/½ cup)
ramekins or moulds.

Place the ramekins in a deep baking dish and
pour enough hot water into the dish to come
halfway up the sides of the ramekins. Bake in
the oven for about 40 minutes, or until the custard
is dry to the touch, but still a little wobbly.
Remove from the oven and allow to cool, before
refrigerating for at least 4 hours — the custard
should be well chilled.

Run a knife around the inside rim of the ramekins
and gently turn out onto four individual plates.
Serve with ice cream or cream.

Avocado is usually used in savoury dishes, but not in Brazil, where I first tasted this exotic custard. It now reminds me of fantastic food, dancing, beaches, jungle, sun and beautiful bodies — not bad for a dessert!

# barefoot on the beach and splendour in the grass

## outdoor food

Everything tastes fresher outdoors and there is no better place to enjoy the bounties of nature than the far north coast. You can choose from umpteen picturesque locations, spread some colourful rugs and tablecloths, get hot, strip off and cool down.

A twilight dinner at the beach is an amazing barbecue experience — think ocean aromas intermingling with the waft of a chargrilled whole fish. Savour chargrilled king prawns as you watch the setting sun's reflections blush the ocean. And complete the picture by adding chilled riesling. Invite loved ones and settle in to share a great picnic rich with fine food and laughter.

The main thing to remember when eating outdoors is to prepare as much as you can in advance and take it with you. That way, as the cook, you can relax and enjoy yourself too!

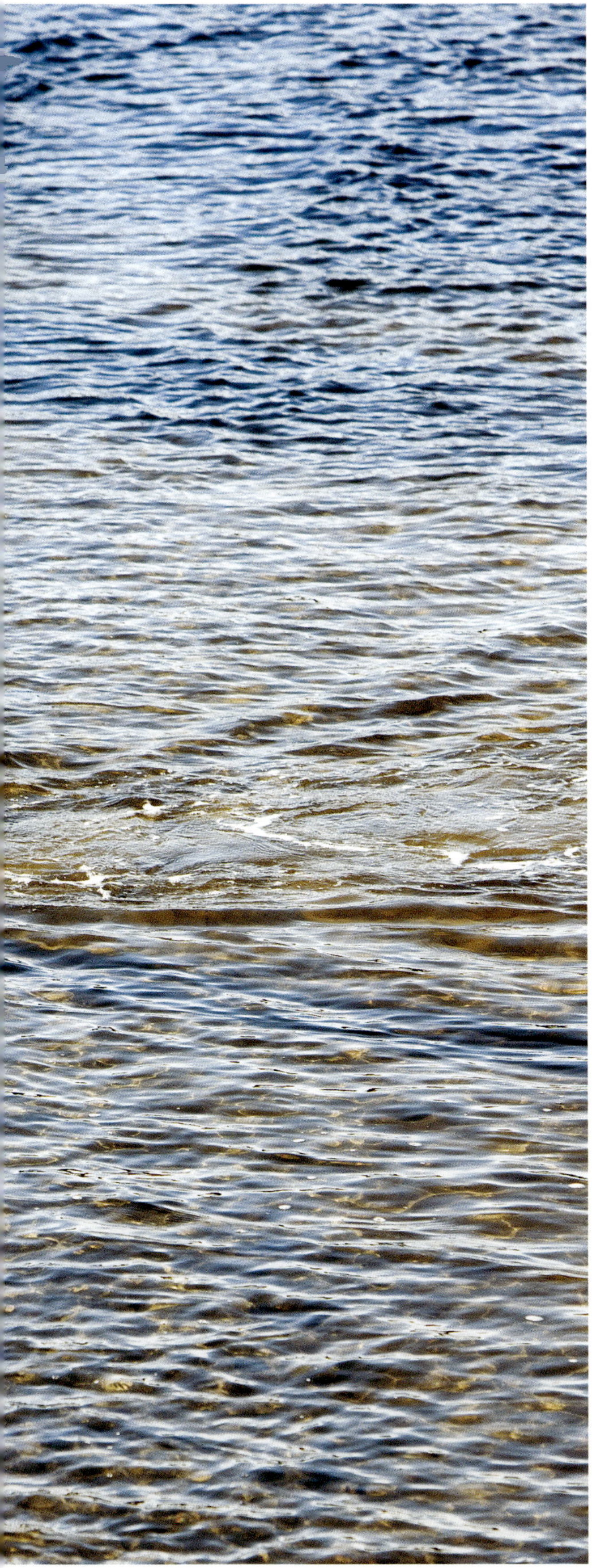

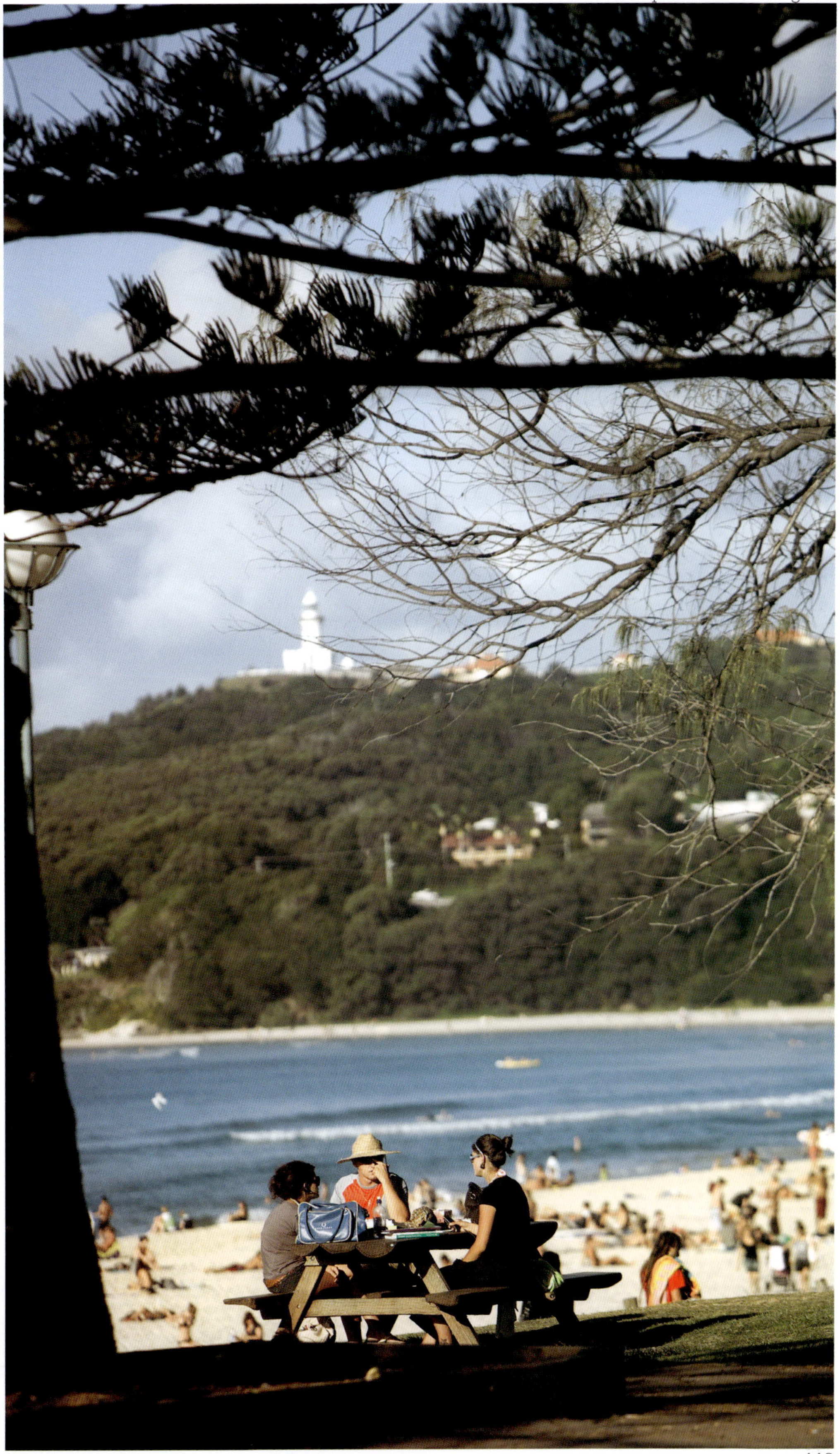

While the beach seems the most obvious place to set up an outdoor feast when you're on the coast, there are also loads of places in hinterland regions just waiting to be explored. A short drive inland from many coastal towns or villages will take you up into lush green hills. Why not pack a picnic basket and set off in the dark to enjoy a sunrise breakfast with stunning views from the mountains to the sea? Wish the fishing trawlers luck as they negotiate their way out into deeper waters to catch prawns and fish (whenever I spot the Brunswick Heads fleet I know some of the catch will undoubtedly end up at Fins). Or make a day trip of it. Load up the car with provisions, family and friends and head for the hinterland national parks and nature reserves. Find your own secluded picnic area backed by waterfalls and set amidst fabulous rainforest. Along the way you are likely to discover quiet little rural villages and their quaint stores and markets offering local produce.

**Be creative with your picnic menus. Tuna steaks and blue-eye trevalla are wonderful on the barbecue — try the teriyaki tuna burger with yuzu mayonnaise (see page 135), most of which is easy to prepare in advance and take with you. If cooking tuna, remember to serve it medium–rare, otherwise it will take on the dryness inherent in tinned tuna. Smoked fish and seaweed salad (see page 122) is also a barbecue favourite, while a barbeued sardine niçoise with preserved lemon mayonnaise (see page 131) is sure to be a hit.**

Use chutneys, salsas, pickles and marinades to lift your dishes out of the ordinary. Try making a Portuguese marinade for a steak or chicken — mix the marinade at home and by the time you're ready to barbecue the flavours will be delicious. Mix ½ teaspoon smoked paprika with 1 cup red wine and 2 crushed garlic cloves, a sprig each of thyme and rosemary, and ½ sliced onion. This marinade will help tenderise the meat. Papaya is the other great tenderising trick. Immerse octopus or cuttlefish in your favourite marinade with some papaya (three strips removed with a peeler). Leave to sit for 4–6 hours before cooking and the flesh will be fall-apart tender. Or try one of my very favourites — chargrilled cuttlefish with chorizo (see page 138).

A picnic can also be a great setting for special occasions, especially during the hotter months. In this part of the world, summer means heat, deafening cicadas and everyone wishing they were by the sea. Keep things simple by basing a picnic menu around the abundance of whatever produce is in season.

When picnicking, sometimes it is easier to stick with cold ingredients, to relieve the pressure of a big production. If everything is served cold, you don't have to worry about timing. Kokoda with a twist (see page 126) is refreshing, clean and easy to make in advance, as is a spicy Chilean scallop ceviche (see page 118). A spiced mud crab and green papaya salad (see page 125) also makes wonderful picnic fare. For the main course, the easiest option is to visit your fishmonger and buy a good selection of cooked, chilled seafood — choose from prawns, smoked fish, oysters, bugs and crab. And let's not forget dessert — an apple, polenta and golden syrup pudding (see page 141) is easily transported and cut up on the beach, as are Portuguese baked apples

(see page 148) — all of which the kids will enjoy eating too.

Fruit is always fantastic any time of year. Cherries, peaches, apricots, mangoes and melons are sensational in the summer months, while pears and apples are great through autumn and winter. Serve everything on platters and let your guests help themselves. Alternatively, serve cherries on shaved ice in a martini glass with a dollop of sour cream sweetened with honey and chopped mint (this sauce is also great with any of the fruits above). You can transform strawberries quickly with a splash of balsamic vinegar and a sprinkle of sugar and black pepper like they do in Morocco.

It doesn't matter if you are having an intimate picnic for two or celebrating a more boisterous occasion — cooking and eating outdoors is always an enjoyable experience. Think about your venue while preparing your menu and make sure you have access to a barbecue if you plan on using one. Oh, and don't forget the bottle opener!

## chilean scallop ceviche

1 tablespoon dried wakame
300 g (10<sup>1</sup>/2 oz) scallops, cleaned (see note)
100 ml (3<sup>1</sup>/2 fl oz) freshly squeezed lemon juice
100 ml (3<sup>1</sup>/2 fl oz) freshly squeezed lime juice
1/2 red onion, finely diced
1/2 tomato, finely diced
1 garlic clove, crushed
1 tablespoon chopped Italian (flat-leaf) parsley
1 tablespoon chopped coriander (cilantro) leaves
1 long red chilli, seeded and julienned, to garnish
1/2 spring onion (scallion), green part only,
    julienned, to garnish
3 cm (1<sup>1</sup>/4 inch) piece of carrot, julienned,
    to garnish

serves 6

Soak the dried wakame in cold water for 5 minutes, then drain and squeeze out any excess moisture. Slice thinly and set aside to use as a garnish.

Slice the scallops in half to create two round, thinner scallops from each. Place in a non-metallic bowl and pour the lemon and lime juices over the top. Cover with plastic wrap and refrigerate for at least 4 hours, stirring occasionally with a wooden spoon.

In a separate bowl, combine the onion, tomato, garlic, parsley and coriander. Add this mixture to the scallops and stir to combine.

Arrange the scallops on a serving platter. Garnish with the combined wakame, chilli, spring onion and carrot, to serve.

note Prise open the scallop shells with a sharp knife — use a cloth to hold the scallops firmly. Lift off the top shell and loosen the scallop from the shell, then pull off and discard the outer grey fringe and membrane. Rinse them quickly under cold running water to remove any sand.

The sweetness of this Asian marinade is fantastic when used in conjunction with smoky chargrilled flavours. Abalone, squid and octopus all work well and can be used instead of prawns if you prefer.

## chargrilled king prawns with asian marinade

24 large raw king prawns (shrimp), peeled and deveined, tails left intact
185 ml (6 fl oz/³/₄ cup) Asian marinade (Basics, see page 222)
green salad, to serve

Serves 8

Place the prawns in the Asian marinade for 1 minute before cooking, then chargrill on a preheated barbecue plate over high heat for 2 minutes on each side, or until the prawns turn pink and start to curl. Serve the prawns with a green salad.

note You can also cook the prawns in a wok over high heat, tossing for 2 minutes, or until they turn pink and start to curl.

# smoked fish and seaweed salad

4 x 70 g (2$^{1}/_{2}$ oz) skinless, boneless firm white fish
    fillets, such as mahi mahi, kingfish or
    blue-eye trevalla
2 teaspoons sesame oil
6 sichuan peppercorns, ground
seaweed salad (Basics, page 229), to serve
$^{1}/_{2}$ carrot, julienned, to garnish
$^{1}/_{2}$ long red chilli, seeded and julienned, to garnish
mint leaves, to garnish
coriander leaves, to garnish

### for smoking

200 g (7 oz/1 cup) jasmine rice
100 g (3$^{1}/_{2}$ oz/$^{1}/_{2}$ cup) soft brown sugar
50 g (1$^{3}/_{4}$ oz/scant $^{2}/_{3}$ cup) gunpowder tea
    (see note)
15 g ($^{1}/_{2}$ oz/scant $^{1}/_{4}$ cup) lemon myrtle tea or
    lemongrass tea

Serves 4

Rub the fish with the combined sesame oil and
ground peppercorns.

Mix all of the smoking ingredients together. Line
the bottom of a wok or large heavy-based frying
pan with aluminium foil and put the smoking
mixture on top. Put the fish on a wire rack over
the smoking mixture, place the wok over high
heat and cover with a lid. Once smoking, smoke
the fish for about 5 minutes, or until it flakes easily
with a fork.

Place a fish fillet on each plate and top with the
seaweed salad. Garnish with the combined carrot,
chilli and herbs. This is a simple dish but can
easily be dressed up for a special occasion
by adding some crispy fried squid.

note Gunpowder tea is a type of Chinese green
tea. Each leaf is rolled to form a small pellet shape
that resembles gunpowder pellets — hence the
name. It is available from Asian grocery stores.

To enjoy sweet crabmeat you need patience — work is required but the reward is awesome. This is a great salad that tastes just as good (and will be slightly cheaper) using spanner crabs.

## spiced mud crab and green papaya salad

1 kg (2 lb 4 oz) live mud crab
4 pieces banana leaf, each cut into 12 x 5 cm
   (4¹/₂ x 2 inch) strips, to serve
green papaya salad (Basics, page 224), to serve
fried Asian shallots, to garnish

Serves 4

Place the crab in the freezer for 30 minutes until it sleeps. Bring a saucepan of water to a gentle simmer and plunge the crab into the pan for 8–9 minutes, or until the shell has turned a bright orange. Immediately plunge the crab into a pan of iced water to stop it cooking further. Drain and allow to cool.

Pull back the flap and remove the top shell of the crab. Discard the gills and rinse the remaining crab. Remove the claws and cut the body into quarters. Crack the claws with the back of a cleaver. Carefully remove all the meat from the crab, keeping the pieces as large as possible. Discard any cartilage and shell.

To serve, place a piece of banana leaf on each plate and top with the crabmeat, reserving 4 tablespoons to toss through the papaya salad. Divide the salad over each plate and garnish with fried Asian shallots.

Kokoda is Fiji's national dish — a ceviche using fish sauce instead of salt. It is hot-weather food that is cool, clean and refreshing to eat — perfect for an outdoor picnic.

## kokoda with a twist

500 g (1 lb 2 oz) skinless, boneless white fish fillets, such as snapper, kingfish, amberjack or blue-eye trevalla
100 ml (3½ fl oz) freshly squeezed lemon juice
100 ml (3½ fl oz) freshly squeezed lime juice
3 tablespoons fish sauce
100 ml (3½ fl oz) fresh coconut milk (see page 101 for extraction method)
1 small red banana chilli, seeds and membrane removed, finely chopped
1 small tomato, finely diced
½ red onion, finely sliced
1 tablespoon chopped flat-leaf (Italian) parsley
1 tablespoon chopped coriander (cilantro) leaves

Serves 4

Cut the fish fillets into 1 cm (½ inch) cubes and place in a non-metallic bowl. Pour the lemon and lime juices over the fish and allow to marinate in the refrigerator for 4 hours, stirring occasionally with a wooden spoon.

Add the remaining ingredients to the fish and gently combine. Serve in glass serving dishes.

### picnics

This recipe is from Büyükada Island in Turkey, where the restaurants display colourful fish kebabs at their entrances, along with salads of fresh tomato, cucumber, dill, parsley and sumac. There are no cars on the island, only horse-drawn carriages, so I had to walk to one of the popular picnic spots on a cliff overlooking the sea. I expected piles of wood to be stacked near the barbecue area, but soon came to understand that in Turkey you have to throw a bag of charcoal in the basket if you want to cook anything. While our party drank wine and water the local Turkish people were drinking raki (a potent aniseed-flavoured spirit). This, and the fact that they were all dressed resplendently in tailored coats, shiny shoes and even traditional robes, was a shock to me. To my delight the atmosphere became even more surreal with an impromptu dance performance accompanied by Turkish guitar. I was brought back to earth as an errant football passed by my head, reminding me that some constants remain in this great and diverse world — there is no escaping loud and boisterous barbecue types no matter where you go!

# mahi mahi kebab

## marinade

3 tablespoons extra virgin olive oil
3 tablespoons freshly squeezed lemon juice
2 garlic cloves, finely chopped
1 small brown onion, sliced
1 teaspoon paprika

1 kg (2 lb 4 oz) skinless, boneless firm white fish
    fillets (about 3 cm/1¼ inch thick), such as
    mahi mahi, blue-eye trevalla or kingfish
8 fresh bay leaves
1 red capsicum (pepper), seeded, membrane
    removed and cut into 3 cm (1¼ inch) squares
2 small zucchini (courgette), sliced
2 slender Japanese eggplants (aubergines), sliced
2 small red onions, cut into thin wedges
8 bamboo skewers, soaked in water for 1 hour
rice pilaf (Basics, see page 229), to serve
lemon and lime wedges, to serve
yoghurt, to serve
fresh mint leaves, chopped to serve
1 teaspoon sumac, to serve

Makes 8

Preheat the oven to 200°C (400°F/Gas 6). Cut the fish into 3 cm (1¼ inch) cubes.

To make the marinade, combine the olive oil, lemon juice, garlic, onion and paprika in a stainless-steel bowl and stir well. Season with sea salt. Add the fish, bay leaves and vegetables to the marinade and coat well. Cover with plastic wrap and refrigerate for at least 4 hours, turning every so often.

Thread the fish and vegetables alternately onto each skewer until all the ingredients are used, making sure there is a bay leaf on each. Reserve the marinade.

Place the skewers on a tray and cook in the oven for 10 minutes, turning once and brushing with the marinade halfway through, until all sides are cooked. If barbecuing, grill the skewers over hot glowing coals, turning the kebabs frequently and brushing occasionally with marinade, for about 10–12 minutes, or until cooked.

Serve the kebabs on the rice pilaf with a dollop of yoghurt that has been sprinkled with the combined mint and sumac.

**anchovies**

In the wild, anchovies occur in Australian waters south of the Tropic of Capricorn; they live and breed in bays and estuaries, feeding on plankton, which is what makes their flesh so soft. In Australia, most anchovies are processed (that is, turned into fish paste, frozen, pickled or packed in salt or brine). While they are not naturally salty, salting has always been the preferred preserving method, which firms the anchovies' flesh. Salted anchovies need to be soaked overnight in water or milk to remove any excess salt before cooking. After washing the salt off, pat them dry, fillet them and use immediately so they don't brown and lose flavour. If, for whatever reason, you can't use them immediately, cover them in olive oil. (If you buy tinned fillets in oil, all this has already been done for you.)

Fresh anchovies are wonderful. Those lucky enough to have access to them should eat them as soon as possible after they are caught, as they deteriorate quickly. To prepare fresh anchovies, use a sharp knife to make an incision along the stomach, remove the guts and rub the scales off with your fingers or a cloth. Rinse and pat dry with paper towel. They should then be marinated in lemon juice or white wine vinegar and olive oil, and used as required.

In Portugal you can go to the wharf and meet the 'pescadors' (or fisherman), who will give you a handful of fresh sardines. On one occasion I shared a breakfast of barbecued sardines and a 5 litre flagon of red wine with a fisherlady — it was a memorable morning!

## barbecued sardine niçoise with preserved lemon mayonnaise

2 cos lettuce, leaves washed and dried
2 waxy potatoes, such as sebago, boiled, quartered and kept warm
200 g (7 oz/1$\frac{1}{3}$ cups) roasted red capsicum (pepper), cut into strips
200 g (7 oz/1$\frac{2}{3}$ cups) green beans, steamed
2 roma (plum) tomatoes, quartered
4 hard-boiled free-range eggs (or quail eggs), quartered and kept warm
1 small red onion, finely sliced
4 black olives, pitted and halved
2 tablespoons extra virgin olive oil
2 tablespoons red wine vinegar
12 anchovy fillets, chopped
16 fresh or good-quality frozen sardine fillets (see note)
100 ml (3$\frac{1}{2}$ fl oz) extra virgin olive oil, for frying (optional)
20 g ($\frac{3}{4}$ oz) butter, for frying (optional)

### preserved lemon mayonnaise
2 egg yolks
1 teaspoon Dijon mustard
200 ml (7 fl oz) vegetable oil
3 tablespoons olive oil
2 tablespoons Champagne vinegar or white wine vinegar
2 tablespoons freshly squeezed lemon juice
$\frac{1}{2}$ piece preserved lemon, zest only, rinsed and finely chopped (Basics, see page 227)
ground white pepper, to taste

Serves 4

Share the lettuce among four plates or bowls. Combine the potatoes, capsicum strips, beans, tomatoes, eggs, onion and olives in a bowl. Combine the oil and vinegar and toss through the vegetable mixture to coat. Season with sea salt and arrange the vegetable mixture over the lettuce leaves. Scatter the anchovy fillets on top.

To make the mayonnaise, place the egg yolks and mustard in a food processor and blend until smooth. With the motor still running, slowly add the combined vegetable and olive oils, very slowly at first, then increase to a slow trickle as the mayonnaise thickens. Add the vinegar, lemon juice and preserved lemon, and blend until combined. Season with white pepper, to taste. Set aside. Any left-over dressing can be refrigerated in a sterilised airtight container for 2–3 days.

Season the sardine fillets with sea salt and cook on a preheated hot chargrill or barbecue plate for 2 minutes each side, or until cooked through. Alternatively, heat the olive oil and butter in a frying pan and add the sardines, cooking for 2 minutes each side.

To serve, arrange four sardine fillets on top of the salad and drizzle generously with the preserved lemon mayonnaise.

note If you prefer, you can reduce the saltiness of the sardines by first marinating them in milk for 1 hour before cooking.

# teriyaki tuna burgers with yuzu mayonnaise

### marinade

250 ml (9 fl oz/1 cup) dark soy sauce
2 garlic cloves, finely chopped
1.5 cm (5/8 inch) piece ginger, finely chopped
175 g (6 oz/1/2 cup) honey
1 bird's eye chilli, finely sliced (optional)

4 x 120 g (41/4 oz) tuna steaks (yellow fin or
    albacore)
1 loaf Turkish bread, cut into 4, then halved
    and toasted
4 tablespoons yuzu mayonnaise (Basics, see
    page 232)
1 carrot, grated
6 cos lettuce leaves, finely shredded
1 small fresh beetroot, grated
1 tomato, finely sliced
1 small handful basil leaves
3 tablespoons peanut oil or vegetable oil
1 teaspoon sesame oil

Serves 4

To make the marinade, put the soy sauce, garlic,
ginger, honey and chilli in a bowl. Whisk together
with 125 ml (4 fl oz/1/2 cup) water, until well
combined. Pour into a shallow, non-metallic
baking dish and add the tuna fillets in a single
layer, ensuring they are covered in the marinade.
Cover with plastic wrap and allow to marinate
for at least 1 hour in the refrigerator.

Spread the toasted Turkish bread with yuzu
mayonnaise, then layer the salad ingredients
and basil on top of four of the slices.

Preheat the barbecue plate to high. Remove the
tuna from the marinade. Mix the peanut and
sesame oils together in a small bowl and brush
over the tuna. Cook the tuna for 1 minute each
side to seal, but making sure it is still rare in the
centre. You can also cook it in a frying pan for
1 minute on each side over high heat.

Serve immediately on the salad-laden Turkish
bread and top with the toasted bread.

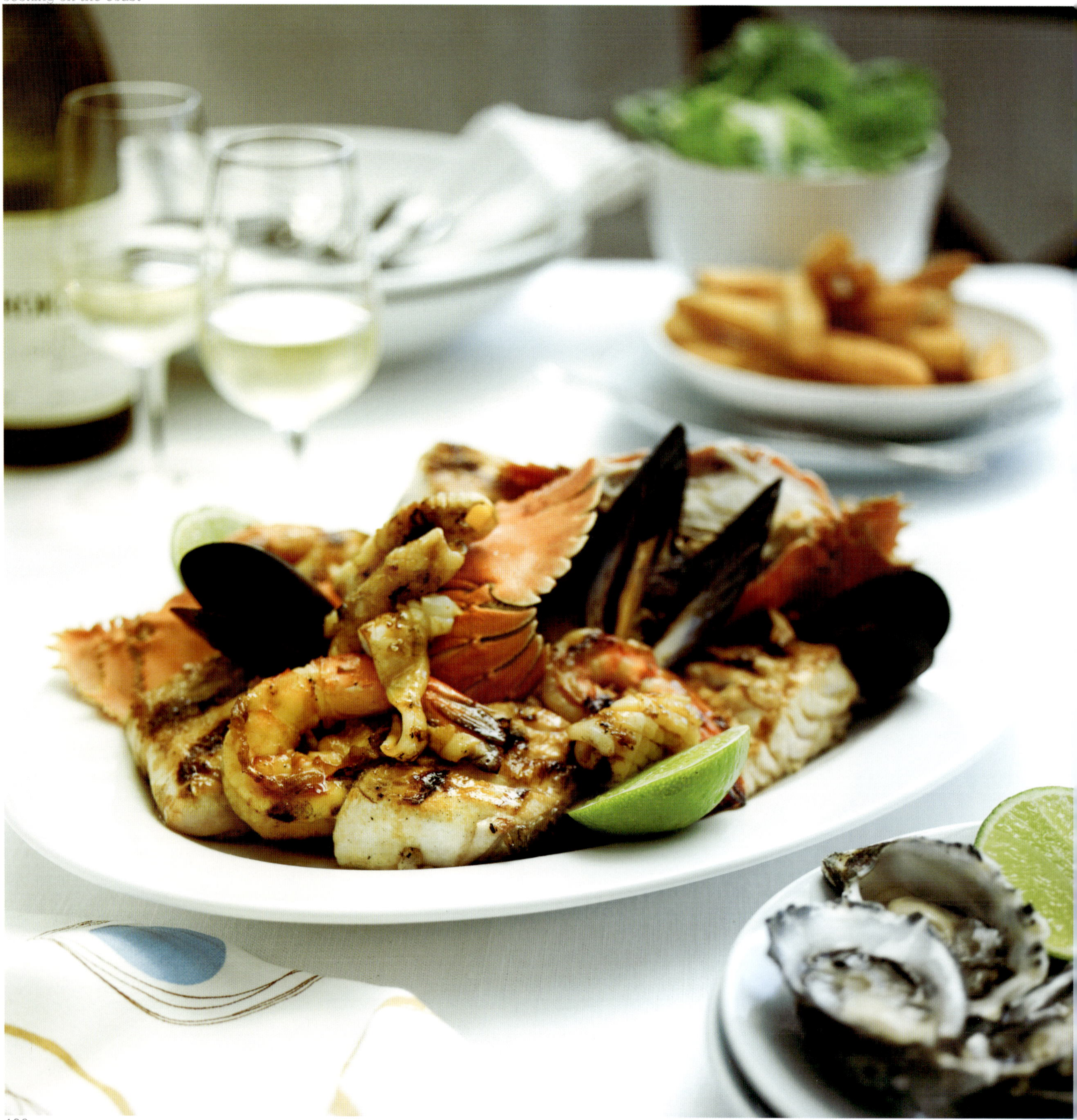

We eat with our eyes first. A good seafood platter is a feast for the eyes, nose and stomach. Choose seafood with a 'wow' factor, like fresh bugs, octopus and fish cooked in different marinades — mixing hot and cold seafoods.

## barbecue seafood platter

### Asian baste

3 tablespoons peanut oil
2 teaspoons sesame oil
125 ml (4 fl oz/1/2 cup) kecap manis
60 ml (2 fl oz/1/4 cup) fish sauce

### seafood platter

4 x 100 g (3 1/2 oz) skinless, boneless snapper
    fillets or sashimi-quality yellow fin tuna
    steaks
8 small cooked bugs
8 black mussels
1 garlic clove, crushed
3 tablespoons white wine
1 tablespoon butter
8 cleaned squid tubes
8 large raw king prawns (shrimp), peeled and
    deveined, tails left intact
8 oysters, on the half shell
lemon or lime wedges, to serve

Serves 4

To make the Asian baste, combine the peanut oil, sesame oil, kecap manis and fish sauce in a large shallow bowl and whisk thoroughly to combine. Place the fish fillets in the marinade and set aside for 10 minutes before cooking.

Cut each bug in half lengthways and remove the intestinal tract. Scrub the mussels with a stiff brush and pull out the hairy beards. Discard any broken mussels, or open ones that don't close when tapped on the work surface. Rinse well.

Preheat the barbecue grill plate to high. Put the mussels in an ovenproof frying pan and add the garlic, wine and butter. Cover with a lid and steam for 5 minutes, or until the mussels open. Discard any mussels that don't open.

Meanwhile, cook the fish fillets on the barbecue plate. If using snapper, cook over high heat for 2 minutes on each side, or until just cooked. If cooking tuna, seal the steaks for 90 seconds on each side, making sure they are still rare in the middle.

Cook the squid tubes and prawns for 2 minutes on each side, basting liberally with the remaining marinade as they cook. Cut the cooked squid into 2 cm (3/4 inch) strips.

Arrange the seafood on a platter with the oysters and serve immediately with lemon or lime wedges for squeezing over.

This one flew back on the aeroplane with me from Portugal — every element adds a different dimension to the finished dish, resulting in a real synergy of flavours. It is perfect for the chargrill and great wine food … anything red from Spain or Portugal.

## chargrilled cuttlefish with chorizo

8 raw cuttlefish (about 400 g/14 oz)
4 kipfler (fingerling) potatoes
2 tablespoons extra virgin olive oil
1 red capsicum (pepper)
2 chorizo sausages, cut on the diagonal
parsley oil (Basics, page 227), to serve

### marinade
50 g (1³/₄ oz) papaya, roughly chopped
1 garlic clove, finely chopped
70 ml (2¹/₄ fl oz) vegetable oil

Serves 4

To prepare the cuttlefish, grasp the body in one hand and the head and tentacles in the other. Pull firmly to separate. Cut the head away and discard. Pull the quill (transparent cartilage) from inside the body and discard. Remove and discard any white membrane, the flaps and tentacles. Pull away the skin under cold running water and cut in half lengthways.

Combine the marinade ingredients and marinate the cuttlefish for at least 3 hours, covered, in the refrigerator.

Cook the potatoes in a saucepan of boiling water over high heat for 20 minutes, or until tender. Halve lengthways, season with sea salt and cracked black pepper and toss in a little extra virgin olive oil.

Cut the capsicum in half, removing the membrane and seeds. Cook, skin side up, under a hot grill (broiler) until the skin blackens and blisters. Remove from the heat, cool in a plastic bag, then peel and cut into thin strips.

Wipe off any excess marinade from the cuttlefish and pat dry with a clean tea towel (dish towel).

Preheat the barbecue grill plate to high. Lay the cuttlefish on the grill and place a weight on top (such as a frying pan), to keep the cuttlefish flat. Cook the cuttlefish for 1 minute on each side, or until cooked through. Meanwhile, add the chorizo to the barbecue grill plate and cook for 2 minutes on each side, or until slightly crispy.

To serve, divide the potatoes and capsicum between four plates. Stack the chorizo, and cuttlefish on top, and garnish with the parsley oil.

This pudding is a take on a traditional semolina pudding with maple syrup. Here I have used polenta instead of the semolina, and added some Australian icons — golden syrup and lemon myrtle. This is all about texture; if cooked too long the pudding will present well but fail the texture test — it should only just stand up when served!

## apple, polenta and golden syrup pudding

1.5 litres (52 fl oz/6 cups) milk
260 g (9¼ oz) caster (superfine) sugar
4 lemon myrtle leaves (2 wide strips of lemon or lime zest can be substituted)
60 g (2¼ oz) butter
225 g (8 oz/1½ cups) fine instant polenta
200 ml (7 fl oz) thick (double/heavy) cream
60 g (2¼ oz/½ cup) sultanas (golden raisins)
200 g (7 oz/1¼ cups) roasted macadamia nuts, chopped
3 granny smith apples, peeled, cored and sliced
350 g (12 oz/1 cup) golden syrup (or ½ cup dark corn syrup combined with ½ cup honey), plus extra, to garnish
ice cream or cream, to serve (optional)

Serves 12

Preheat the oven to 160°C (315°F/Gas 2–3). Grease a 25 cm (10 inch) spring-form cake tin and line the base and side with baking paper.

Put the milk in a saucepan over medium heat and add 200g (7 oz) of the sugar, the lemon myrtle leaves and butter. Bring to the boil, then remove from the heat and stand for 15 minutes to allow the lemon myrtle to infuse. Strain the milk mixture and discard the myrtle leaves.

Return the milk to the pan and reduce the heat to low. Add a pinch of salt and then stir in the polenta in a steady stream and cook for about 20 minutes — you will need to stir constantly to ensure the mixture has a smooth consistency. Remove from the heat and add the cream, sultanas and macadamia nuts, stirring well to combine.

Pour the polenta mixture into the prepared tin. Arrange the apple slices in an overlapping pattern on top of the cake and then drizzle over the golden syrup. Sprinkle the remaining caster sugar on top and bake in the oven for 45 minutes, or until the top of the cake has browned and is slightly wobbly. This cake is best eaten slightly undercooked.

Remove from the oven and allow to cool in the tin. Drizzling over a little golden syrup, then cut into wedges and serve with ice cream or cream.

I first fell in love with cannoli in a beautiful little café in Sicily — after returning again and again to pester the owner for the recipe I came up with this adaptation. It is the perfect dessert to serve with coffee.

## cannoli morgana

### brandy snap pastry

100 g (3<sup>1</sup>/<sub>2</sub> oz) unsalted butter, softened
90 g (3<sup>1</sup>/<sub>4</sub> oz/<sup>3</sup>/<sub>4</sub> cup) plain (all-purpose) flour
90 g (3<sup>1</sup>/<sub>4</sub> oz/<sup>1</sup>/<sub>2</sub> cup) caster (superfine) sugar
100 g (3<sup>1</sup>/<sub>2</sub> oz/<sup>1</sup>/<sub>4</sub> cup) golden syrup (dark corn syrup)

### filling

400 g (14 oz/1<sup>2</sup>/<sub>3</sub> cups) ricotta cheese
50 g (1<sup>3</sup>/<sub>4</sub> oz/<sup>1</sup>/<sub>3</sub> cup) soft goat's curd
100 g (3<sup>1</sup>/<sub>2</sub> oz/<sup>3</sup>/<sub>4</sub> cup) icing (confectioners') sugar
1 tablespoon very finely grated mandarin zest
<sup>1</sup>/<sub>2</sub> teaspoon orange-blossom water
<sup>1</sup>/<sub>2</sub> teaspoon natural vanilla extract
a pinch ground cinnamon
30 g (1 oz/<sup>1</sup>/<sub>4</sub> cup) finely chopped unsalted pistachio nuts
golden syrup, to garnish (optional)

Serves 8

Preheat the oven to 160°C (315°F/Gas 2–3). Lightly grease two baking trays and line with baking paper.

Place the softened butter in a bowl and add the flour, caster sugar and golden syrup. Beat together until a smooth paste forms.

Take 1 tablespoon of the mixture at a time and, using your hands, roll into eight small balls. Place two balls each on the prepared trays, with about 12 cm (4<sup>1</sup>/<sub>2</sub> inches) space between each, allowing room for them to spread during cooking.

Bake in the oven for 3–5 minutes, then remove and allow to cool slightly. While still warm, mould each pastry disc around a cannoli mould or thin rolling pin, to form a cone or cylinder shape. Allow to cool for a minute on the mould, then slide off and allow to cool completely. Repeat with the remaining four balls.

To make the filling, combine the ricotta, goat's curd and icing sugar in a bowl and beat with a wooden spoon until as smooth as possible. Add the mandarin zest, orange-blossom water, vanilla, cinnamon and pistachio nuts, and combine well.

Just before serving, spoon or pipe the mixture into the cannoli tubes until they are almost filled. Drizzle with a little golden syrup and serve.

# baked ricotta tart

150 ml (5 fl oz) Frangelico
220 g (7³/₄ oz/1 cup) pitted prunes

### pastry

180 g (6¹/₂ oz) chilled butter, diced
250 g (9 oz/2 cups) plain (all-purpose) flour
1 egg yolk
3 tablespoons iced water

### ricotta filling

125 g (4¹/₂ oz) butter, melted
230 g (8¹/₂ oz/1 cup) caster (superfine) sugar
3 eggs
250 g (9 oz/1 cup) sour cream
500 g (1 lb 2 oz/2 cups) ricotta cheese
poached fruit, to serve (optional)

Serves 8

Put the Frangelico in a saucepan over medium heat and bring to the boil. Add the prunes and enough hot water to just cover them. Bring to the boil, then reduce the heat and simmer for 5 minutes. Remove from the heat and allow the prunes to steep in the syrup for at least 3 hours.

Preheat the oven to 180°C (350°F/Gas 4). Lightly grease eight individual 10 cm (4 inch) round loose-based fluted tartlet tins.

To make the pastry, use your fingertips to lightly rub the butter into the flour until the mixture resembles coarse breadcrumbs. Add the egg yolk and stir with a flat-bladed knife, adding the iced water if necessary. When the mixture starts to come together in small beads, gently gather together into a ball and knead the dough a couple of times on a lightly floured surface. Flatten into a disc, cover with plastic wrap and refrigerate for 30 minutes.

Roll out the pastry between two sheets of baking paper to 5 mm (¹/₄ inch) thickness. Cut circles large enough to fit the base and side of the tins. Gently press the pastry into each tartlet tin and trim any excess pastry overhanging the edge. Lightly prick the bases with a fork. Refrigerate for 30 minutes.

Line each pastry shell with a square of lightly crumpled baking paper and pour in some baking beads or uncooked rice. Bake for 10 minutes, remove the paper and beads and return to the oven for a further 5 minutes, or until lightly golden. Remove from the oven and cool. Lower the oven temperature to 160°C (315°F/Gas 2–3).

To make the ricotta filling, put the butter, sugar, eggs, sour cream and ricotta in a food processor and blend until smooth. Cut the prunes almost in half, leaving them hinged, and open out. Place the prunes, cut side down, in the pastry cases to cover the base. Divide the ricotta filling over the top of each. Bake in the oven for 20 minutes, or until set.

Remove from the oven and allow to cool completely before refrigerating for at least 2 hours. Serve cold, with poached fruit, such as pears, or extra prunes if desired.

note Any left-over prunes can be stored in an airtight container in the refrigerator for 1 week. You can also cook one large tart — use a round 25 cm (10 inch) loose-based fluted flan (tart) tin, about 3 cm (1¼ inch) deep. Cook for about 30–35 minutes, or until set.

These apples are easy to take on a picnic and enjoy outdoors. They are homely, rustic and work well on their own or with yoghurt, cream or ice cream.

## portuguese baked apples

60 g (2¼ oz/½ cup) raisins
125 g (4½ oz/1¼ cups) walnuts, toasted
3 tablespoons honey
a large pinch cinnamon
4 granny smith apples, cored
40 g (1½ oz) butter, melted
175 g (6 oz/¾ cup) caster (superfine) sugar
125 ml (4 fl oz/½ cup) Madeira or port wine
pouring (whipping) cream or vanilla ice cream,
    to serve

Serves 4

Preheat the oven to 180°C (350°F/Gas 4). Grease and line a baking dish with baking paper.

Grind the raisins and walnuts together in a mortar, using a pestle to form a rough paste. Transfer to a bowl and stir in the honey and cinnamon to form a sticky mass. Roll the paste into four logs that are just smaller than the holes left by the apple cores and pack the mixture into each apple.

Sit the apples upright in the baking dish. Brush with the butter and place a tablespoon of sugar on top of each, followed by a splash of Madeira. Bake in the oven for about 30 minutes, or until the apples are tender and caramelised. Remove from the oven and serve warm or at room temperature on individual plates with cream or vanilla ice cream, if desired.

# night sky and sparkling slip-ons
## cooking in the restaurant

When I first arrived in Byron Bay to operate the Railway Friendly Bar I remember being asked by a newly employed local chef what type of food I intended to do. I answered pastas, risottos and other things, to which he replied, 'None of that trendy Sydney rubbish will work here, mate.' I also remember compiling our fruit and vegetable order and asking for eggplant. Our fruiterer informed me that if I wanted to order any 'exotics' he would need a week's notice!

After stints at a few other local haunts, including the Piggery (now known as the Arts Factory) and the magnificent Brunswick Heads Hotel, I decided to purchase a bankrupt restaurant with a bad reputation. It was called Fins and located on a bend in the Brunswick River. It had been closed for six months and was considered a 'jinxed' site by locals. The building closely resembled a bomb shelter, but once you stepped out of the back door you were greeted with the most amazing river and mango-tree vista. The only problem was, you were also eaten alive by sandflies. This was my beginning at Fins.

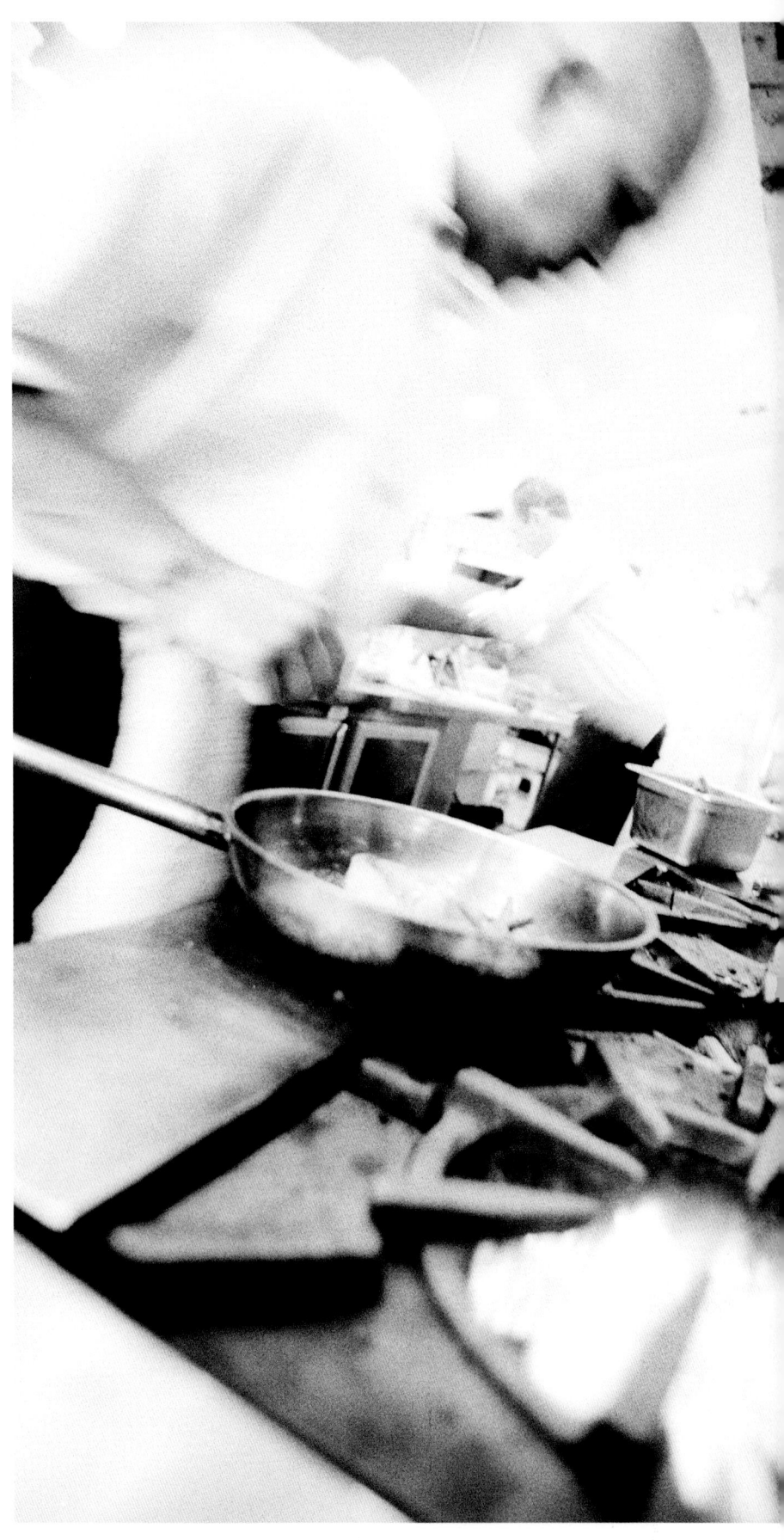

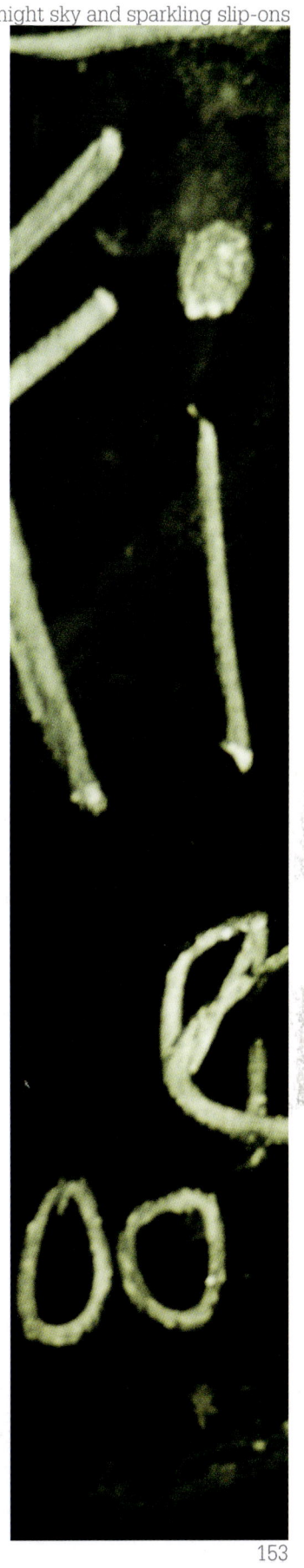

We scrubbed and cleaned every wall in that Brunswick Heads restaurant and bought 'pre-loved' equipment from defunct Sydney venues, mixing it with a few domestic things from home. The manager at the Brunswick co-op was perplexed that I would order octopus, squid and pipis that he knew as 'by catch'. By catch meant all the stuff (other than prawns) dredged up by prawn trawlers. He thought of it as bait, and in fact the only other guy interested in it ran the local bait shop. While eating 'by catch' was popular in places like France and Portugal, in Brunswick Heads I had customers voicing major reservations. To some, eating chargrilled octopus served with potatoes and a simple dressing was unthinkable — I would have got a better reception serving it to non-human flatheads.

**Fins at Brunswick was quirky — the front staff would set the outside tables with a complimentary bottle of insect spray so customers were armed to do battle with the sandflies. Even so, there were famous people, High Court judges, local folk out for special occasions and others bribing our waiters to secure a table. There were colourful racing identities and people celebrating the harvest of a great 'crop' (local speak for making heaps of money**

**selling dope). Our outside dining area was both scenic and problematic. People would complain about our resident python sliding between tables during service. (We simply moved them to a less snake-infested area.) The shade of the mango tree was pleasant, however, mangoes tended to fall. On one occasion a mango happened to drop on the head of a very prominent local romance novelist, which didn't go down well at all. Similarly, the resident water rats were not interested in observing the demarcation zone (our outside dining room) and on some nights could be spotted doing victory laps around the floor.**

People were funny too. One lunch almost all the punters 'full of the joys of life' decided to remove their clothes for reasons best known only to them. They proceeded to dive into the river out the back while others ran across the Brunswick Bridge (in fact the Pacific Highway) in the nude. I then became the target. When the customers in the restaurant next door began to complain the manager attempted to wrap tablecloths around anyone she could catch.

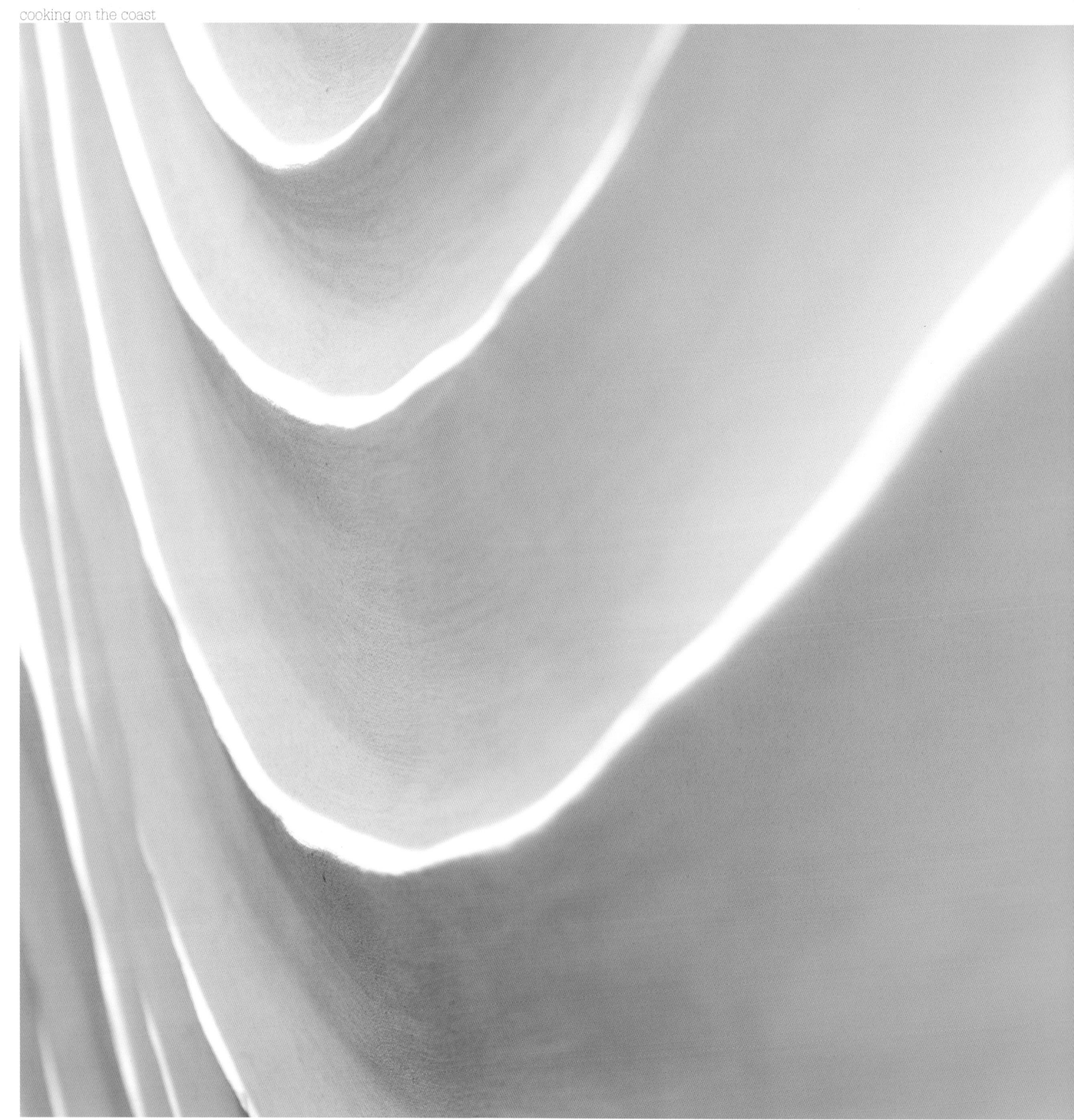

Fins was winning awards and notoriety. People would fly from Sydney for the weekend while locals had permanent bookings. Even so, eventually everything comes to an end and after eight years, the RTA re-routed the highway and our doors closed. At this stage Fins had two chef's hats and was awarded the best restaurant outside Sydney by the *Sydney Morning Herald Good Food Guide*. We also won the best seafood restaurant in NSW with the Restaurant and Caterers Association.

At this point I reached an agreement with John and Delvene Cornell to take over the restaurant at their iconic architectural masterpiece, The Beach Hotel at Byron Bay. Fins Byron was a major step up in class from Brunswick. At Byron we retained two chef's hats for the duration of our tenure, as well as winning best regional restaurant most years. Our food was refined, the punters loved it and we met interesting folk. Over the seven years I ran the business at The Beach Hotel I travelled the world as a guest chef, got divorced, lost money, won it back, was blessed with a daughter and set course on a new life involving meditation, food combining and yoga. In fact, all the new-age 'Byron hippie things' I would previously have laughed at became my modus operandi.

We now served food on expensive plates and I had excellent chefs from near and far adding their professional touches to the food. This gave me an opportunity to work with the best in the business. Guys like Geoff Lindsay, Neil Perry, Yamamoto, Hideki 'Eki' Takegi, Armando Percuoco, Tetsuya, Janni Kyritsis and Martin Boetz all cooked at Fins. During this time both Byron and Fins changed profoundly. When the Cornells sold the property in 2007 I saw it as time for a new challenge and looked north to Salt Village at South Kingscliff where I had been planning to open the newest Fins.

Restaurants are taxing and addictive and my new restaurant, half an hour up the road from Byron Bay, was a chance to design my ultimate dining venue. As well as a fine-dining restaurant it has a sexy tapas bar and a takeaway service to boot. It is still by the sea, our fish are still line-caught and the menu similar. We have a united nations of chefs, a grand sommelier and plenty of things Portuguese. Sunday lunch is back and I am cooking most nights after doing fish deals at 6 am. In this chapter you will find the signature dishes from the menu that make the name 'Fins' great.

## cod

To prepare fresh cod for salting, coat the fish completely with rock salt in a non-metallic dish. Cover and place in the refrigerator for at least 48 hours — once salted, the cod is 'preserved' and can be stored in the refrigerator for long periods of time.

To desalinate the cod before cooking is easy, but requires a few days to complete. Thoroughly rinse the fish under cold running water to wash off the salt, then place it in a non-metallic dish and cover with fresh water. Allow to soak overnight before repeating the rinsing and soaking process twice more, refreshing the water each time, until the water no longer tastes salty. The cod is then ready for cooking.

# bacalao balls

125 ml (4 fl oz/$^1$/$_2$ cup) extra virgin olive oil
2 brown onions, finely sliced
2 garlic cloves, finely chopped
250 g (9 oz/1 cup) desalinated salt cod
    (see side note)
2 floury potatoes, boiled and mashed
125 ml (4 fl oz/$^1$/$_2$ cup) pouring (whipping) cream
45 g (1$^1$/$_2$ oz/$^1$/$_2$ cup) grated Parmigiano Reggiano
    cheese
1 egg, lightly beaten
250 ml (9 fl oz/1 cup) milk
125 g (4$^1$/$_2$ oz/1 cup) plain (all-purpose) flour
90 g (3$^1$/$_4$ oz/1$^1$/$_2$ cups) panko (Japanese
    breadcrumbs)
vegetable oil, for deep-frying

Makes 24 balls

Heat the oil in a frying pan over medium heat. Add the onion and garlic and cook for 3 minutes, or until the onion has softened. Break up the cod (making sure you remove any bones) and add to the pan. Cook for 5 minutes, continuing to break it up into smaller flakes with the back of a fork. Add the mashed potato to the pan and gently cook for 10 minutes, stirring constantly. Make sure you continue to lift any residue sticking to the bottom of the pan as it will add flavour. Add the cream and stir to combine, then add the grated cheese and stir through. Remove from the heat and season with sea salt and cracked black pepper, to taste. Cool slightly.

Stir together the egg and milk in a bowl. Scatter the flour on one plate and the breadcrumbs on another. Take 1 tablespoon of the mixture at a time and roll into balls until you have 24 balls in total. Lightly coat each ball first with the flour, then the egg wash mixture, and roll to coat the entire surface in breadcrumbs. Place on a tray lined with baking paper and refrigerate for at least 1 hour.

Fill a deep-fryer or large heavy-based saucepan one-third full of oil and heat to 180°C (350°F). Deep-fry the balls in batches, for about 3–4 minutes each batch, or until crisp and golden. Drain on paper towels and serve hot.

## finger limes

Finger limes are native limes from the sub-tropical rainforests of northern New South Wales. They get their name from their irregular shape, which is said to resemble a finger. They are seasonal fruit with a distinctive flavour and vary in colour from light green to yellow, pink, light red and deep magenta.

When shucking oysters, the aim is to open the shell and preserve the precious liquid inside. To open an oyster you will need a shucking knife or a small screwdriver, and a little practice perfecting the technique.

## natural oysters with ponzu sauce and finger lime

### ponzu sauce

3 tablespoons freshly squeezed lemon juice, strained
125 ml (4 fl oz/1/2 cup) rice wine vinegar
80 ml (2 1/2 fl oz/1/3 cup) light soy sauce
1 1/2 tablespoons mirin
1 tablespoon finely grated orange zest
a large pinch of bonito flakes

36 unshucked Sydney rock or Pacific oysters
crushed ice, to serve
coarse salt, to serve
3 finger limes, plus extra, to garnish

Makes 36

To make the ponzu sauce, put the lemon juice, vinegar, soy sauce, mirin and orange zest in a saucepan over high heat and bring to the boil. Add the bonito flakes and remove from the heat. Stand for 3 minutes, then strain the liquid. Allow to cool and set aside until needed.

Hold each oyster with a tea towel (dish towel) and insert the point of the knife into the hinge that holds the two shells together. Lever between the shells gently with an up and down motion until the oyster 'pops'. Run the knife around the rim of the oyster and remove the top shell. Cut the muscle of the oyster, located two-thirds down the shell, and carefully turn the oyster in its shell, trying to keep as much of the natural oyster liquid as possible. Wipe the oyster shell clean, being careful to remove any broken pieces. Repeat with the remaining oysters.

Divide the crushed ice and salt onto six serving plates and arrange 6 oysters on the half shell on each, with a piece of finger lime to garnish in the centre. Using a teaspoon, drizzle a small amount of ponzu dressing over each oyster. Squeeze some of the finger lime juice over the top and serve immediately.

note Any extra ponzu sauce can be stored in the refrigerator for 2 weeks. It is also excellent served with sashimi.

# fragrant lobster in lettuce cups

1 kg (2 lb 4 oz) cooked rock lobster
4 dried shiitake mushrooms
80 ml (2$^1$/$_2$ fl oz/$^1$/$_3$ cup) peanut oil
1 tablespoon sesame oil
8 red Asian shallots, finely chopped
2 garlic cloves, finely chopped
2 teaspoons yellow bean sauce
3 teaspoons oyster sauce
3 tablespoons fish sauce
6 tinned water chestnuts, chopped
6 tinned baby bamboo shoots, chopped
$^1$/$_2$ Lebanese (short) cucumber, peeled, seeded
    and diced
2 spring onions (scallions), cut into 2 cm
    ($^3$/$_4$ inch) lengths
3 basil leaves, torn into small pieces
8 mint leaves, cut into small pieces
2 fresh makrut (kaffir lime) leaves, very finely
    sliced
80 g (2$^3$/$_4$ oz/$^1$/$_2$ cup) peanuts, toasted and finely
    chopped
1 tablespoon freshly squeezed lime juice
1 large mango, flesh diced into small cubes
1 iceberg lettuce, leaves trimmed with scissors
    to form cups, and chilled well
3 tablespoons dried Asian shallots

Serves 8–12

To remove the lobster tail, grasp the head and body with two hands and twist firmly in opposite directions to release the tail. Using kitchen scissors, cut down both sides of the shell on the underside and peel back the shell. Gently pull out the flesh in one piece. Gently pull out the vein and cut the lobster into small bite-sized pieces. Refrigerate until needed.

Soak the shiitake mushrooms in boiling water for 45 minutes. Squeeze out any excess moisture. Discard the stems and finely slice the caps.

Heat the peanut and sesame oils in a wok over medium–high heat. Add the red shallots and garlic and fry for 2 minutes, or until golden. Add the mushrooms and cook for 2 minutes. Add the yellow bean, oyster and fish sauces and stir thoroughly. Stir in the water chestnuts, bamboo shoots, cucumber and spring onions. Add the lobster and simmer for 3 minutes. Add the basil, mint and lime leaves, the peanuts and lime juice and stir through.

Remove from the heat and add the mango. Mix thoroughly. Spoon the filling into the individual lettuce cups. Scatter the dried Asian shallots over the top of each cup and serve.

I still get excited about fresh fish. Just about every night of the week I eat sashimi. Raw fish is so healthy and moreish. At Fins there is always a variation of this sashimi dish on the menu for dinner.

# tuna misaki

### misaki dressing

100 ml (3½ fl oz) sake
100 ml (3½ fl oz) mirin
250 ml (9 fl oz/1 cup) Japanese soy sauce
60 ml (2 fl oz/¼ cup) dashi stock (Basics,
    see page 230)

300 g (10½ oz) sashimi-grade tuna fillet in one
    piece, trimmed into a neat rectangle
1 banana leaf, cut into four 20 cm (8 inch) squares,
    to serve
½ small daikon, julienned using a mandolin
½ small carrot, julienned using a mandolin
pickled ginger, to serve
wasabi paste, to serve

Serves 4 as an entrée

To make the misaki dressing, put the sake and
mirin in a saucepan over high heat and bring to
the boil. Add the soy sauce and dashi and bring
back to the boil. Plunge the tuna into the stock
for 10 seconds. (Only the very outer layer of
tuna should be cooked.) Remove the tuna and
immediately plunge into a bowl of iced water
to arrest the cooking process. Leave for about
10 seconds, then remove.

Wrap the tuna in a clean tea towel (dish towel)
and leave to rest for 5 minutes. Unwrap and place
in a bowl, pour the misaki dressing over the top,
and leave to marinate for 20 minutes, turning
occasionally. Using a sharp knife, cut the tuna
into 3 mm (⅛ inch) slices.

To serve, place a square of banana leaf on each
plate. Divide the tuna pieces between each plate
and arrange the tuna so it is slightly overlapping.
Place the daikon and carrot on the side and
garnish with pickled ginger and wasabi.

note If fresh tuna has to be stored, wrap it in
cheesecloth (muslin) and leave it in the coldest
part of the refrigerator for up to 2 days. Some
people like to wash their fresh fish under the tap
before storing or cooking it, but I don't think
tap water should be used to clean saltwater fish
because it speeds deterioration of the flesh and
removes the natural fish juices.

## crispy oysters with wasabi pickled ginger

30 unshucked Pacific oysters
vegetable oil, for deep-frying
500 ml (17 fl oz/2 cups) tempura batter (Basics,
    see page 231)
wasabi paste, to serve
pickled ginger, julienned, to serve
Japanese soy sauce, to serve

Serves 6

To shuck the oysters, hold each oyster with a tea towel (dish towel) and insert the point of the knife into the hinge that holds the two shells together. Lever between the shells gently with an up and down motion until the oyster 'pops'. Run the knife around the rim of the oyster and remove the top shell. Cut the muscle of the oyster, located two-thirds down the shell, and carefully remove the oyster from its shell. Repeat with the remaining oysters, wiping any excess liquid out of the shells. Place five clean shells on each plate.

Fill a deep-fryer or wok one-third full of oil and heat to 180ºC (350ºF). Working in batches, dip the oysters into the tempura batter and then plunge the oysters into the hot oil for about 30 seconds at a time, or until golden. (The batter needs to be as cold as possible for the best results. Try to dip the oysters in the batter before the ice melts. If the ice melts between batches then you may need to add a little more flour.)

Drain the oysters on paper towels and return to the cleaned shells. Smear a very small amount of wasabi onto each oyster and top with pickled ginger. Serve immediately, with soy sauce on the side for dipping.

I love oysters so much I could inhale them. These have a crunchy tempura batter with unique Japanese flavours and taste delicious!

This squid casserole really deserves fresh squid. For the best result only use a wine that you would be prepared to drink.

## squid and white wine casserole

800 g (1 lb 12 oz) squid
120 ml (3½ fl oz) olive oil
2 brown onions, finely sliced
3 garlic cloves, finely sliced
2 fresh bay leaves
2 carrots, finely sliced
½ chorizo sausage, sliced
250 g (9 oz/1 cup) tinned chopped tomatoes
1 tablespoon tomato paste
    (concentrated purée)
330 ml (11¼ oz/1⅓ cups) riesling, or other dry
    white wine
3 all-purpose potatoes, such as desirée or pontiac,
    peeled and cut into 2.5 cm (1 inch) cubes
200 g (7 oz) green beans, sliced
1 handful flat-leaf (Italian) parsley,
    roughly chopped
Tabasco sauce (optional)
steamed white rice, to serve

Serves 6

Grasp the body of each squid in one hand and the head and tentacles in the other. Pull firmly to separate. Cut the head and tentacles off and discard. Pull the quill (transparent cartilage) from inside the body of the squid and discard. Remove and discard any white membrane. Under cold water, pull away the skin. Cut each squid into 3 cm (1¼ inch) square pieces.

Heat the oil in a saucepan over high heat. Add the onion, garlic, bay leaves, carrot and chorizo and cook, stirring often, for 8 minutes, or until golden brown. Add the squid and cook for 2 minutes, then add the tomatoes and tomato paste and cook for 2 minutes. Add the wine and potatoes and season with sea salt, to taste. Bring to the boil, then reduce the heat and simmer for 25 minutes. Add the beans and cook for a further 5 minutes, or until the beans and squid are tender. Adjust the seasoning and add the parsley and a few drops of Tabasco, if desired. Remove from the heat and serve with steamed white rice.

# pumpkin velouté with crabmeat and parsley oil

800 g (1 lb 12 oz) fresh blue swimmer or spanner crab (about 180–200 g/6$\frac{1}{2}$–7 oz crabmeat)
420 ml (14$\frac{1}{2}$ fl oz/1$\frac{2}{3}$ cups) chicken stock (Basics, see page 231)
40 g (1$\frac{1}{2}$ oz) butter
30 ml (1 fl oz) olive oil
1 large brown onion, finely sliced
1 garlic clove, crushed
300 g (10$\frac{1}{2}$ oz) jap or kent pumpkin (winter squash), finely sliced
3 tablespoons thick (double/heavy) cream (optional)
parsley oil (Basics, see page 227), to serve

Serves 12 as a canapé

Place the crab in the freezer for 30 minutes or until it sleeps (do not freeze completely). Drop it into a large saucepan of boiling water. Reduce the heat and simmer for about 8 minutes, or until bright orange all over—it should be cooked through by this stage. Plunge immediately into a bowl of iced water to halt the cooking process.

Lift the small flap on the underside of the crab and prise off the top hard shell. Remove the soft internal organs and pull off the grey feathery gills. Using a large, sharp knife, cut the crab lengthways through the centre of the body, to form two halves with the legs attached. Cut the crab in half again, crossways. Remove the meat and refrigerate until needed.

Put the chicken stock in a saucepan over high heat and bring to the boil.

Meanwhile, melt the butter and olive oil in a frying pan over medium heat and lightly cook the onion and garlic for 5 minutes, or until soft but not coloured. Add the pumpkin and continue to cook for 5 minutes, or until softened. Add the hot chicken stock and continue to cook for about 20 minutes, or until the pumpkin is very tender. Remove from the heat and allow to cool slightly.

Transfer the soup to a food processor and blend until smooth. Pass the soup through a sieve, then return to the warm saucepan and bring to the boil. Remove from the heat and stir through the cream, if desired.

To serve, divide the crabmeat into the bottom of twelve shot glasses. Pour the hot soup over the crab to almost fill each glass and finish with a drizzle of parsley oil.

# piri piri prawns

### lemongrass stock
375 ml (13 fl oz/1¹/₂) cups chicken stock (Basics,
    see page 230)
185 ml (6 fl oz/³/₄ cup) dry white wine
2 lemongrass stems, lightly bruised
3 teaspoons plain (all-purpose) flour
3 teaspoons butter, melted and cooled

### piri piri marinade
100 ml (3¹/₂ fl oz) freshly squeezed lemon juice
150 ml (5 fl oz) extra virgin olive oil
¹/₂ small red bird's eye chilli, seeded and
    finely sliced
1 garlic clove, finely chopped
2 teaspoons Tabasco sauce
¹/₂ teaspoon cayenne pepper

16 large raw king prawns (shrimp), peeled and
    deveined, tails left intact
3 tablespoons extra virgin olive oil
1 garlic clove, finely chopped
¹/₂ teaspoon finely chopped chilli
1 teaspoon Tabasco sauce
2 baby bok choy, trimmed and blanched, to serve
steamed rice, to serve

Serves 4

Piri piri means chilli in Portuguese. These prawns are chilli hot, acidic, clean-flavoured and perfumed with lemon myrtle to make a wonderful meal.

To make the lemongrass stock, combine the chicken stock, wine and lemongrass in a saucepan over high heat and bring to the boil. Reduce the heat and simmer gently for about 10 minutes. Remove the lemongrass. Season with sea salt. In a separate bowl, combine the flour and melted butter. Whisk through the hot stock until the mixture thickens slightly. Remove from the heat and set aside.

To make the piri piri marinade, combine the lemon juice, olive oil, chilli, garlic, Tabasco sauce and cayenne pepper in a bowl. Toss the prawns in the marinade and set aside for about 5 minutes.

Heat the oil in a frying pan over medium heat, add the garlic and chilli and cook for 30 seconds, being careful not to brown the garlic. Add the prawns and Tabasco, season with sea salt and toss to combine. Add 250 ml (9 fl oz/1 cup) lemongrass stock to the pan and cook for a further 2 minutes, or until the prawns turn pink and start to curl.

Divide the rice between four plates. (In the restaurant we use a ramekin or similar mould to do this.) Arrange the bok choy and prawns next to the rice and drizzle over any pan juices.

# steamed scallops sashimi tower with spiced pumpkin and beetroot

### tamarind dressing
100 ml (3½ fl oz) tamarind water (Basics, see page 231)
1 tablespoon light soy sauce
1½ tablespoons mirin
2 teaspoons freshly squeezed lemon juice

### beetroot reduction
250 ml (9 fl oz/1 cup) fresh beetroot (beet) juice
1 tablespoon red wine vinegar

### pumpkin salsa
3 tablespoons peanut oil
1 tablespoon sesame oil
300 g (10½ oz) jap or kent pumpkin (winter squash), cut into 5 mm (¼ inch) cubes
2 garlic cloves, crushed
3 cm (1¼ inch) piece ginger, finely sliced
3 tablespoons fish sauce
3 tablespoons kecap manis
80 ml (2½ fl oz/⅓ cup) tamarind purée
1 teaspoon caster (superfine) sugar
3 tablespoons finely chopped coriander (cilantro) leaves

### sashimi tower
2 tablespoons sesame oil
2 tablespoons Japanese soy sauce
2 tablespoons mirin
200 g (7 oz) sashimi-grade tuna fillets, finely diced
200 g (7 oz) sashimi-grade firm white fish fillets, finely diced
2 nori (seaweed) sheets

18 scallops, on the shell
seaweed salad (Basics, see page 229), to serve
125 ml (4 fl oz/¼ cup) coconut cream, to serve
2 tablespoons salmon roe, to serve

Serves 6

To make the tamarind dressing, put all of the ingredients in a small saucepan over medium–high heat and simmer for 10 minutes to reduce the liquid to a coating consistency.

To make the beetroot reduction, put the beetroot juice and vinegar in a small saucepan over medium heat and boil for 10 minutes, or until the liquid has thickened slightly.

To make the pumpkin salsa, heat the peanut and sesame oils in a frying pan over medium heat and sauté the pumpkin for 2 minutes. Add the garlic and ginger and cook for a further 2 minutes, or until soft. Add the fish sauce, kecap manis and tamarind purée. Cook for 5 minutes or until the pumpkin is tender, but firm. Add the sugar and coriander and stir through. Set aside and keep warm.

To make the sashimi tower, combine the sesame oil, soy sauce and mirin in a bowl. Divide into two small bowls. Add the tuna to one bowl and the white fish to the other. Stir each to coat the fish.

Cut each nori sheet into six circles with a 3 cm (1¼ inch) diameter. Cut any left-over nori into thin julienne strips and reserve to use as a garnish.

To create the sashimi towers you will need six PVC moulds (i.e. pieces of PVC pipe with a 3 cm (1¼ inch) diameter cut into 4.5 cm (1¾ inch) lengths). Spoon enough tuna into each mould to create a 1 cm (½ inch) thick base. Layer a nori round over the tuna. Next, spoon in a 1 cm (½ inch) thick layer of white fish and top with a nori round. Repeat the layering once more to create the towers, leaving the top layer nori-free. Press the layers down firmly, using a Tabasco bottle or similar.

Meanwhile, to prepare the scallops, prise open the scallop shells with a sharp knife — use a tea towel (dish towel) to hold the scallops firmly. Lift off the top shell and loosen the scallop from the shell, then pull off and discard the outer grey fringe and membrane. Rinse them quickly under running water to remove any sand. Clean six of the bottom shells and set aside until ready to serve.

Place the scallops in a bamboo steamer over a wok or saucepan of rapidly boiling water. Steam the scallops for 2 minutes, or until they turn opaque.

To serve, fill six cleaned half-shells with the seaweed salad and arrange three scallops over the top. Drizzle the tamarind sauce over each scallop, followed by 1 tablespoon of coconut cream over each half-shell. Remove the mould from the sashimi tower and sit alongside the scallops, garnishing with a heaped teaspoon of salmon roe and the reserved nori. Serve with pumpkin salsa on the side and a drizzle of beetroot reduction.

This is an entrée with a real 'wow' factor. It combines different textures, the sourness of tamarind and the flavours of fresh local fish and scallops, all offset by pumpkin and beetroot. I pull this dish out to impress when I am travelling as a guest chef, and it never fails to please. It tastes great with a glass of sparkling shiraz.

# peruvian sashimi with hot shallot oil and chilli

### shallot oil
3 tablespoons extra virgin olive oil
5 red Asian shallots, finely sliced

300 g (10¹/₂ oz) sashimi-grade firm white fish
    fillets, such as mackerel or blue-eye trevalla
1 tablespoon chopped coriander (cilantro) leaves
1 small tomato, seeds removed and finely diced
¹/₄ red onion, finely diced
3 tablespoons olive oil
1 small potato, cut into 5 mm (¹/₄ inch) cubes
1 lime, cut in half
1¹/₂ tablespoons light soy sauce
¹/₂ small fresh red chilli, very finely chopped
6 chives, cut into 2 cm (1 inch) lengths

Serves 4

To make the shallot oil, heat the extra virgin olive oil in a frying pan over low–medium heat and lightly fry the shallots for 8 minutes, or until golden. Set aside.

Put the fish pieces in the freezer for 10 minutes, or until quite firm. Be careful to make sure it doesn't freeze.

Using a very sharp knife, slice the fish into 3 mm (¹/₈ inch) thick slices and lay on a chilled platter, in an overlapping pattern. Scatter the coriander leaves over the top, then sprinkle with the diced tomato and red onion. Season with sea salt and ground white pepper.

Heat the oil in a frying pan over medium–high heat and fry the potato for 6 minutes, or until golden and just cooked. Sprinkle over the fish. Squeeze over lime and then drizzle over the soy sauce. Scatter the chilli and chives on top.

Reheat the shallot oil over medium–high heat until it is sizzling and drizzle over the fish, to serve.

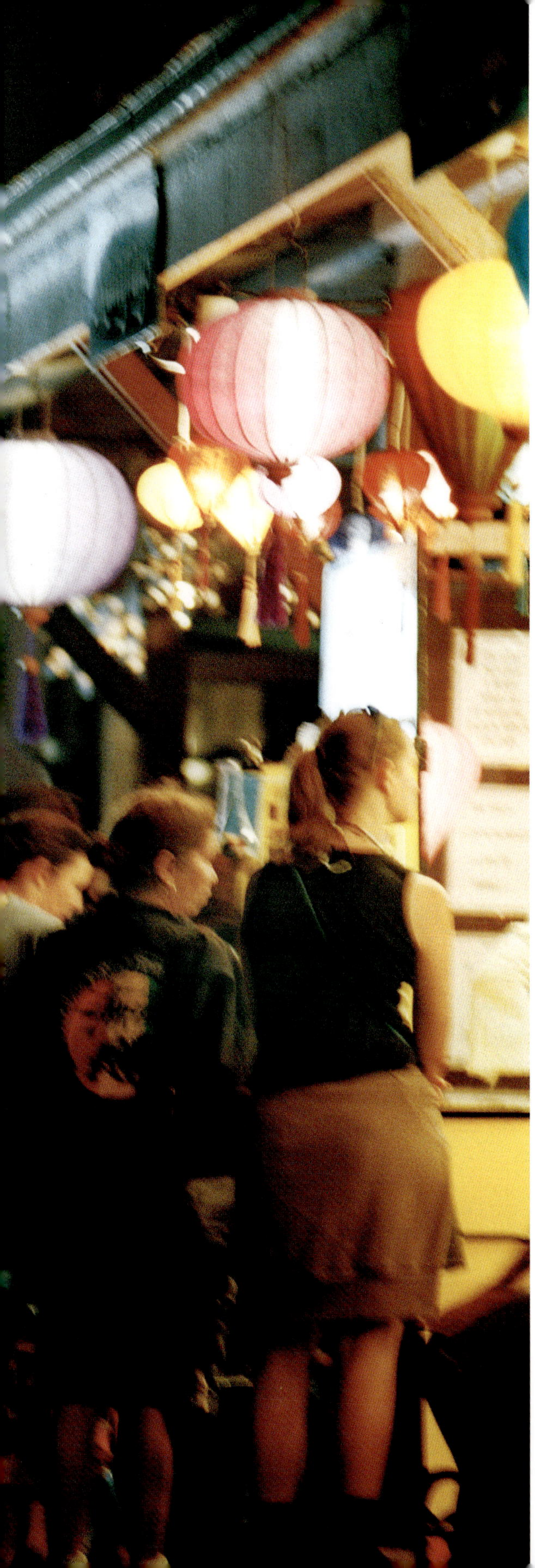

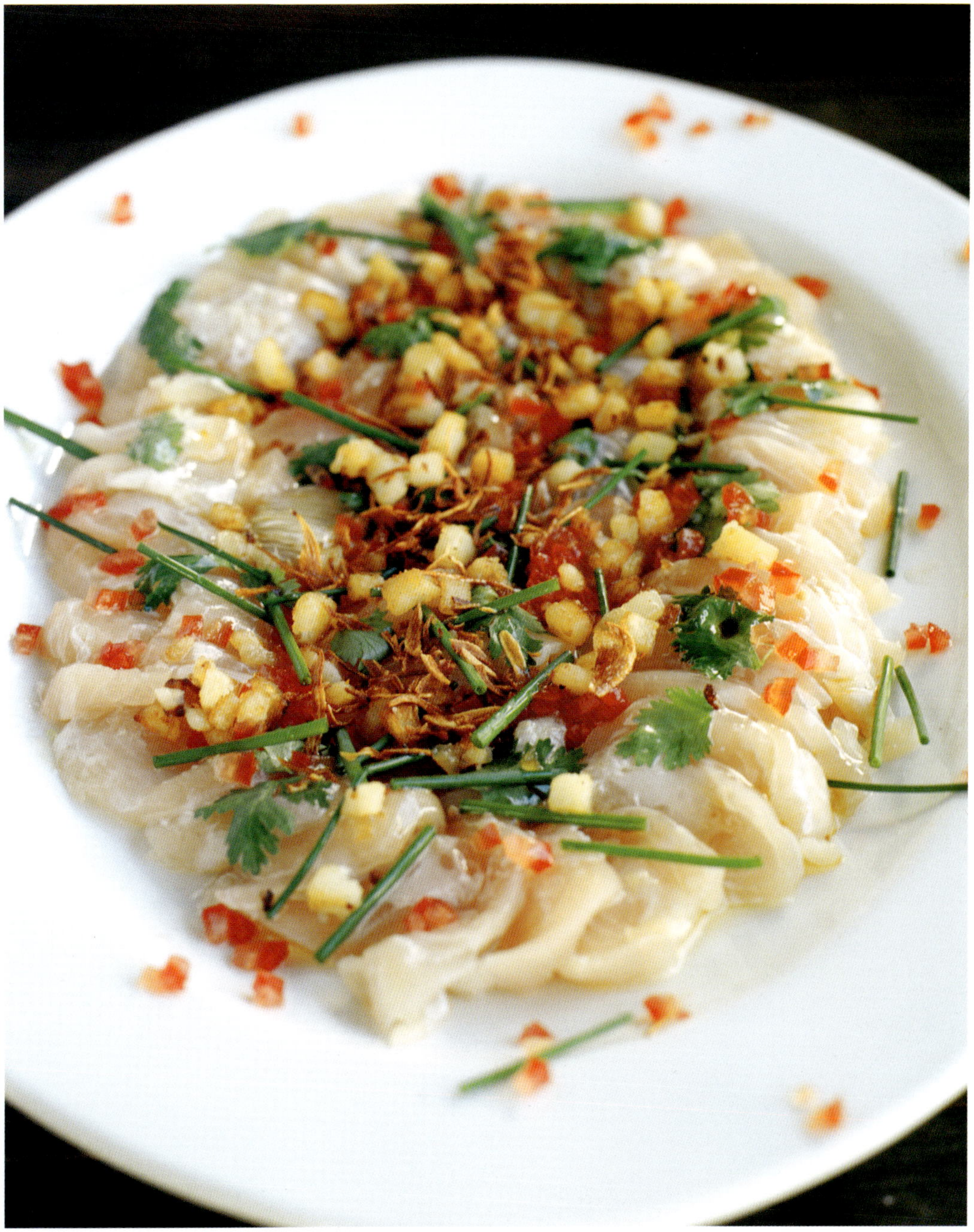

Using organic free-range pork from a trusted local supplier will ensure the meat does not contain antibiotics or growth hormones. As well as being tender and juicy it will also be good for you and the environment. Pork goes well with the prawns and salsa, which provide contrasting textures and flavours enlivened with chilli.

# korean-style barbecue pork, brunswick prawns and green mango papaya salad

### green mango papaya salad
1 green mango, julienned
1 very small green papaya, julienned
3 baby radish, julienned
12 snow peas (mangetout), trimmed and julienned
20 coriander (cilantro) leaves
20 mint leaves
2 French shallots, finely sliced
2 tablespoons nam jim (Basics, see page 226)

### barbecue pork marinade
55 ml (1³/₄ fl oz) hoisin sauce
1¹/₂ tablespoons shaoxing rice wine
1¹/₂ tablespoons oyster sauce
1 tablespoon tamarind purée
1 tablespoon light soy sauce
1 tablespoon fish sauce

2 litres (70 fl oz/8 cups) master stock (Basics, see page 230)
1 kg (2 lb 4 oz) boneless pork belly in one piece
16 large prawns (shrimp), peeled and deveined, tails left intact
125 ml (4 fl oz/¹/₂ cup ) Asian marinade (Basics, see page 222)
2 limes, quartered, to serve
2 tomatoes, cut into 1 cm (¹/₂ inch) thick slices, to serve
8 chives, cut in half, to garnish

Serves 8

To make the green mango papaya salad, put all the ingredients in a bowl and toss to combine in the nam jim dressing. Cover with plastic wrap and refrigerate until ready to serve.

To make the barbecue pork marinade, combine all the ingredients together in a bowl and mix well. Refrigerate until needed.

Bring the master stock to the boil in a large saucepan over medium heat. Add the pork belly, reduce the heat and gently simmer for 3 hours, or until the pork is very tender. Lift the pork belly from the stock and reserve the stock for another use (it is great for poaching fish).

Cut the pork into strips about 10 cm (4 inches) in length and 2 cm (³/₄ inch) thick. Place them in a single row on a tray lined with baking paper. Place a weighted tray over the top and refrigerate for at least 4 hours, or overnight.

Cut the compressed pork in half again to create 5 cm (2 inch) lengths. Brush the pork belly with the barbecue pork marinade to glaze. Preheat the barbecue plate to hot. Cook for 2 minutes on each side, or until crispy. Place the prawns on the chargrill plate and brush with the Asian marinade on both sides. Cook the prawns for 2 minutes on each side, or until they turn pink and start to curl. Remove from the heat and brush with the Asian marinade, to coat.

To serve, put two slices of tomato on each plate and season with sea salt. Place a piece of pork on each tomato slice and top each with a prawn. Arrange the green mango papaya salad on top. Serve with a lime wedge and garnish with the chives.

## mud crab tempura in chilli yuzu sauce with fish spätzele salad

6 x 100 g (3$\frac{1}{2}$ oz) soft-shell mud crabs
rice flour, for coating
vegetable oil, for deep-frying
500 ml (17 fl oz/2 cups) tempura batter (Basics, see page 231)
yuzu mayonnaise (Basics, see page 232), to serve
parsley oil (Basics, see page 227), to serve

### crab marinade

1$\frac{1}{2}$ tablespoons shaoxing rice wine
1 tablespoon fish sauce
1 tablespoon peanut oil
1 teaspoon sesame oil
3 makrut (kaffir lime) leaves
3 large red chillies, seeded
3 cm (1$\frac{1}{4}$ inch) piece ginger, chopped
50 g (1$\frac{3}{4}$ oz/$\frac{1}{3}$ cup) grated palm sugar (jaggery)

### fish spätzele salad

150 g (5$\frac{1}{2}$ oz) skinless, boneless firm white fish fillet, such as blue-eye trevalla, chopped
1 egg white
finely grated zest of 1 lemon
1 heaped tablespoon rice flour
25 g (1 oz) butter
55 ml (1$\frac{3}{4}$ fl oz) pouring (whipping) cream
ground white pepper, to taste
60 g (2$\frac{1}{4}$ oz) daikon, cut into 1 cm ($\frac{1}{2}$ inch) cubes
1 tablespoon chopped flat-leaf (Italian) parsley
3 tablespoons preserved lemon dressing (Basics, see page 227)

Serves 6

Using a large sharp knife, cut the crabs through the centre of the body to form two halves with the legs attached. Gently peel back the shell, leaving some connective tissue and the shell intact. Carefully remove the feathery gills and intestines and discard. Replace the shells to their original starting point and set aside.

This is a great dish because all the individual elements come together to create a wonderful synergy. It was first made at Fins during the time the talented Phil Woolaston was head chef.

To make the marinade, place all of the marinade ingredients into a food processor with 100 ml (3¹/₂ fl oz) water and blend until as smooth as possible. Transfer to a large bowl and add the crab halves, tossing to coat in the marinade. Cover with plastic wrap and refrigerate for at least 30 minutes.

To make the fish spätzele, place the fish, egg whites, lemon zest, rice flour, butter and cream into a food processor and season with sea salt and ground white pepper. Blend until smooth.

Put 1 litre (35 fl oz/4 cups) water in a saucepan over high heat and bring to the boil. Place a colander with 6 mm (¹/₄ inch) drain holes over the boiling water. Push the fish mixture through the colander holes with the back of a large spoon so they fall into the boiling water and form noodles. Gently remove the noodles from the water as they float — this will take about 1 minute. Plunge into a bowl of iced water to arrest the cooking process, then drain quickly and place in a warmed bowl. Cover to keep warm.

In a double-boiler, steam the daikon cubes for 4 minutes, or until cooked through. Add the daikon, parsley and preserved lemon dressing to the noodles and toss gently to combine.

Fill a deep-fryer or wok one-third full of oil and heat to 180°C (350°F). Dip the crab into the rice flour, shaking off any excess, then into the tempura batter. Deep-fry in batches for about 3 minutes, or until golden and cooked through. Remove from the oil with a slotted spoon and drain on paper towels. Season with sea salt.

To serve, drizzle the yuzu mayonnaise and parsley oil over a serving plate. Arrange the spätzele salad on the plate, place the crab over the top and serve immediately.

# chargrilled crayfish with champagne and finger lime foam

2 x 800 g (1 lb 12 oz) fresh or frozen crayfish
250 ml (9 fl oz/1 cup) fish stock (Basics, see
    page 230)
250 ml (9 fl oz/1 cup) Champagne
250 ml (9 fl oz/1 cup) pouring (whipping) cream
2 finger limes or the finely grated zest of 1 lime
55 ml (1³/₄ fl oz) milk, chilled

Serves 2

Immobilise the live crayfish in the freezer for
1 hour. If using frozen crayfish, defrost. Turn each
crayfish upside down, insert a knife through the
shell between the legs and cut first through the
tail, then rotate and continue to cut along through
the head. Separate each crayfish to get four
halves. Wash the shells under cold running water
to remove any residue from the head.

Put the fish stock in a saucepan over high heat
and bring to the boil. Add the Champagne,
reduce the heat and simmer for 15 minutes.
Add the cream and continue to simmer for
10 minutes, or until the liquid has reduced
by half. Add the juice of 1 finger lime and stir
to combine.

Allow to cool slightly before transferring the
liquid to a food processor and blending for
2 minutes, or until a bubbling foam forms. Add
the milk and continue to blend (this will help to
create more bubbles).

Meanwhile, preheat the barbecue plate to high.
Place the crayfish, shell side down, on a chargrill
plate and cook for 4 minutes. Turn and cook the
other side for 2 minutes, or until the meat turns
opaque and is cooked through. Arrange the
crayfish halves on serving plates. Scoop the foam
bubbles off the top of the liquid and spoon over
the crayfish. Squeeze some finger lime pulp over
the top to garnish and serve.

## cataplana

Like many great dishes this one was originally peasant food. The seafood that Portuguese fishermen's wives could not sell at market was transformed into the family meal with the addition of 'fillers', such as onions, garlic, potatoes, tomatoes and (because they are Portuguese) wine. Everything was placed into a cataplana, heated and eaten. In Portugal, cataplanas are served with fish entrails, skate wings and heads of things pescatorial I have not met anywhere near the Pacific. However, the flavours are marvellous.

At Fins we have removed the entrails, added saffron, line-caught fish, bugs, the best king prawns in the world, local squid and pipis, plus a few other tricks, to serve something far removed from its peasant origins but with its soul intact.

A cataplana is a metal cooking dish that locks on the side so it can be turned upside down for even cooking.

This is a signature dish at Fins but works equally as well at home and is great to serve at dinner parties. The fresh seafood tastes wonderful poached in an aromatic light saffron and wine-infused stock with a hint of anise.

## cataplana of seafood

### cataplana sauce

125 ml (4 fl oz/1/2 cup) extra virgin olive oil
2 brown onions, finely sliced
2 garlic cloves, finely sliced
8 anchovy fillets, chopped
2 tablespoons lisbon paste (Basics, see page 226)
4 fresh bay leaves
375 ml (13 fl oz/1 1/2 cups) dry white wine
500 g (1 lb 2 oz/2 cups) tinned chopped tomatoes
1 litre (35 fl oz/4 cups) chicken stock (Basics, see page 230)
a pinch saffron threads, steeped in 250 ml (9 fl oz/1 cup) hot water for 20 minutes
1 teaspoon caster (superfine) sugar
10 drops Tabasco sauce
2 star anise

12 black mussels
6 x 70 g (2 1/2 oz) skinless, boneless firm white fish fillets, such as mahi mahi, jewfish or snapper
6 fresh or frozen raw bugs
6 small cleaned squid tubes
12 king prawns (shrimp), peeled and deveined, tails left intact
6 scallops, on the half-shell
2 tablespoons extra virgin olive oil
1 brown onion, finely sliced
1 garlic clove, finely sliced
1 tablespoon lisbon paste (Basics, see page 226)
2 potatoes, peeled, boiled and cut into 1 cm (1/2 inch) slices
1 fresh bay leaf
chopped flat-leaf (Italian) parsley, to garnish (optional)

Serves 6

To make the cataplana sauce, put the olive oil in a large saucepan over medium–high heat. Add the onion, garlic, anchovy, lisbon paste and bay leaves and sauté for 8–10 minutes, or until the onions are golden. Add the wine and tomatoes and bring to the boil.

Add the stock, saffron water, sugar, Tabasco and star anise to the pan and season with sea salt and cracked black pepper. Reduce the heat and simmer gently for 30–40 minutes, to cook out the raw flavours. Remove from the heat and adjust the seasoning if required.

Meanwhile, prepare the seafood. Scrub the mussels with a stiff brush and pull out the hairy beards. Discard any broken mussels, or open ones that don't close when tapped on the work surface. Rinse well. Turn each bug upside down. Insert a large knife through the shell between the legs, cutting through and along the tail. Slice the squid tubes in half to open and then cut each into quarters.

Heat the oil in a saucepan over medium–high heat. Add the onion, garlic, lisbon paste, potatoes, bay leaf and mussels and cook for 1 minute. Add the fish and toss well to coat in the oil. Add the cataplana sauce and continue cooking for 3 minutes. Add the bugs and cook for 1 minute. Add the squid and prawns and cook for 1 minute. Add the scallops and cook for a further 1–2 minutes, or until they turn opaque and the prawns turn pink and start to curl. Return the scallops to clean half-shells to serve and garnish with parsley.

# red poached fish with asian vegetables

4 x 165 g (5³/₄ oz) boneless firm white fish fillets,
    such as blue-eye trevalla or bar cod

### poaching liquid
100 ml (3¹/₂ fl oz) mushroom soy sauce
100 ml (3¹/₂ fl oz) light soy sauce
200 ml (7 fl oz) shaoxing rice wine
1.5 cm (⁵/₈ inch) piece of ginger, finely sliced
2 garlic cloves, crushed
50 g (1³/₄ oz/¹/₄ cup) raw (demerara) sugar
1 piece cassia bark or 1 cinnamon stick
2 tablespoons finely sliced orange zest
2 dried shiitake mushrooms
1 star anise
500 ml (17 fl oz/2 cups) fish or chicken stock
    (Basics, see page 230)

### asian vegetables
1 tablespoon peanut oil
¹/₂ teaspoon sesame oil
2 spring onions (scallions), peeled and julienned
1 garlic clove, finely chopped
1.5 cm (⁵/₈ inch) piece ginger, julienned
¹/₂ long red chilli, julienned
4 oyster mushrooms, finely sliced
20 g (³/₄ oz/1 cup) snow pea (mangetout) sprouts
90 g (3¹/₄ oz/1 cup) bean sprouts
1 bunch bok choy (pak choy), chopped
100 g (3¹/₂ oz/³/₄ cup) green beans, finely sliced
100 g (3¹/₂ oz/1 cup) snow peas (mangetout)

Serves 4

To make the poaching liquid, put the soy sauces, rice wine, ginger, garlic, sugar, cassia bark or cinnamon stick, orange zest, shiitake mushrooms and star anise in a large, deep frying pan over high heat and bring to the boil. Lower the heat and simmer for 10 minutes. Add the stock and return to a simmer until needed.

Meanwhile make the Asian vegetables. Put the peanut and sesame oils in a wok or large heavy-based frying pan over high heat, swirling to coat the base and sides. Add the spring onion, garlic, ginger and chilli, then all the vegetables, and cook, stirring, for 2 minutes, or until just starting to become tender. Remove from the heat and keep warm.

Gently lower the fish fillets into the simmering stock and poach for 4 minutes, or until slightly undercooked (the flesh will be a pearl colour rather than white); the fish will continue to cook after it is removed from the broth.

To serve, share the Asian vegetables among four plates and place the fish on top. Spoon about 3 tablespoons of poaching liquid over each fish fillet and serve immediately.

# moroccan fish tagine

### tagine sweet potatoes

150 ml (5 fl oz) extra virgin olive oil
1 brown onion, finely sliced
2 garlic cloves, finely chopped
300 g (10¹/₂ oz) sweet potato, cut into 2.5 cm
    (1 inch) cubes
1 teaspoon Moroccan spice (Basics, see page 226)
90 g (3¹/₄ oz/¹/₃ cup) tinned chopped tomatoes
50 g (1³/₄ oz/¹/₄ cup) pitted dates, halved
1 tablespoon preserved lemon, rinsed and finely
    chopped (Basics, see page 227)
80 ml (2¹/₂ fl oz/¹/₃ cup) dry white wine

16 green beans, trimmed
4 x 150 g (5¹/₂ oz) thick boneless, skinless white
    fish fillets, such as mahi mahi, snapper, pig
    fish, jewfish, leatherjacket or flathead
ground white pepper, to taste
a pinch Moroccan spice (Basics, see page 226)
60 g (2¹/₄ oz/¹/₂ cup) plain (all-purpose) flour
3 tablespoons extra virgin olive oil
3 tablespoons dry white wine
4 tablespoons chermoula (Basics, see page 222)
8 pitted kalamata olives, halved
1 handful flat-leaf (Italian) parsley, finely chopped,
    to serve
1 handful mint leaves, finely chopped, to serve
80 g (2³/₄ oz/1 scant cup) toasted flaked almonds,
    to serve

Serves 4

To make the tagine potatoes, heat the oil in a frying pan over medium heat. Add the onion and garlic and sauté for 5 minutes, or until lightly golden. Add the potato and Moroccan spice, and cook for 3 minutes, stirring to combine. Add the tomatoes, dates, preserved lemon and wine. Cover the pan and simmer for 30 minutes over low heat, or until the potato is tender. Keep warm until ready to serve

Put the green beans in a saucepan of salted boiling water and blanch for 2 minutes, or until tender. Drain and set aside.

Season the fish fillets with sea salt and ground white pepper. Sprinkle each fillet with a pinch of Moroccan spice and dust with the flour. Heat the olive oil in a large frying pan over medium heat and cook the fish for 1½ minutes on each side, or until lightly coloured. Add the wine and cook for 1 minute. Evenly spread the chermoula over the top of each fish fillet. Add the olives and green beans and continue to cook for a further 2–3 minutes, or until the fish is almost cooked in the centre. Remove from the heat.

To serve, share the tagine sweet potatoes between four plates. Place a fish fillet on top of the potatoes and arrange the green beans and olives over the fish. Sprinkle the parsley and mint into the pan juices and swirl to combine, then drizzle over the fish. Garnish with the toasted flaked almonds.

One Sunday lunch at Fins in Brunswick Heads, a local real estate agent ordered the Mauritian sambal, which features octopus. He ate everything else in the dish but could not cop the integral ingredient — octopus. He proceeded to thread the octopus onto a fishing line he had retrieved from his car and cast it from his riverside table. Incredibly, he very quickly caught a huge flathead and roamed the restaurant showing off his catch.

This was unusual, but the weirdest event occurred on a busy Friday night. In the midst of service a fisherman banged on our kitchen door saying he had just dragged a dead guy from the river and wanted to leave him in our outside dining area (which was packed with our Friday night crowd). I was too busy and stressed to react, so was thankful when a couple of staff members dealt with the situation and made an attempt, albeit unsuccessful, to resuscitate him.

# mauritian seafood sambal with lotus-wrapped rice

400 g (14 oz) skinless, boneless firm white
    fish fillets, such as blue-eye trevalla, cobia,
    leatherjacket or mahi mahi
12 live mussels or pipis
6 raw bugs
6 small cleaned squid tubes
6 large raw king prawns (shrimp), peeled and
    deveined, tails left intact
green papaya salad (Basics, see page 224),
    to serve

## sambal

5 cardamom pods, seeds only
1/2 teaspoon fenugreek seeds
100 ml (3 1/2 fl oz) peanut oil
1 tablespoon sesame oil
1 brown onion, finely sliced
2 garlic cloves, finely sliced
2.5 cm (1 inch) piece ginger, finely sliced
3 small fresh red chillies, seeded and sliced
3 tablespoons red curry paste (Basics, see
    page 228)
300 g (10 1/2 oz) baby octopus, cleaned
300 g (10 1/2 oz/1 1/4 cups) tinned chopped tomatoes
55 ml (1 3/4 fl oz) fish sauce
55 ml (1 3/4 fl oz) kecap manis
500 ml (17 fl oz/2 cups) chicken stock (Basics,
    see page 230)
1 lemongrass stem, bruised and tied in a knot
100 ml (3 1/2 fl oz) coconut milk

## lotus-wrapped rice

200 g (7 oz/1 cup) jasmine rice
3 tablespoons sesame oil
1 lemon myrtle leaf
1 dried lotus leaf

Serves 6

Cut the fish fillets into 24 bite-sized pieces. Scrub the mussels with a stiff brush and pull out the hairy beards. Discard any broken mussels, or open ones that don't close when tapped on the bench. Rinse well. Turn the bugs upside down. Insert a large knife through the shell between the legs and cut through the head. Cut through one side of each squid to open it out flat and then cut into four even quarters.

Preheat the oven to 180°C (350°F/Gas 4). To make the sambal, scatter the cardamom and fenugreek seeds on a baking tray and toast in the oven for 3 minutes, or until fragrant. Grind in a mortar, using a pestle, until powdery.

Combine the peanut and sesame oils in a large saucepan over medium heat. Add the onion, garlic, ginger, chilli, curry paste and ground spices and cook for 7 minutes, or until golden, stirring occasionally. Add the octopus, tomato, fish sauce and kecap manis. Cook for 5 minutes, stirring to combine. Add the stock, increase the heat, and bring to a boil. Reduce the heat and simmer for 20 minutes. Add the lemongrass and simmer for a further 20 minutes, then add the coconut milk and simmer for 1 minute. Turn off the heat.

To make the lotus-wrapped rice, rinse the rice under cold running water until the water runs clear. Place in a heavy-based saucepan over high heat and add the sesame oil, lemon myrtle leaf and 375 ml (13 fl oz/1 1/2 cups) water. Bring to the boil. Season with sea salt and reduce to a gentle simmer, leaving the lid tightly sealed. Cook for a further 10 minutes. Remove from the heat and rest for 10 minutes.

Soak the lotus leaf in cold water for 30 minutes. Remove the leaf and pat dry. Remove the stem and cut the leaf into quarters. Lay each quarter on a flat surface and place 120 g (4 1/4 oz/2/3 cup) of cooked rice in the centre of each leaf piece and roll into a cone. Fold the base over to form a flat base so the cone can stand upright on the plate.

Just before you are ready to serve, bring the sambal sauce back to the boil. Add the fish, mussels and bugs for 3 minutes, then add the squid and prawns and cook for a further 2 minutes, or until the seafood is almost cooked. (The seafood will continue to cook when removed from the heat.) Discard any mussels that do not open.

To serve, place the lotus-wrapped rice on each plate. Arrange 2 tablespoons of green papaya salad next to the rice. Spoon the seafood sambal into bowls and serve with the rice and salad.

Tamarin Bay in Mauritius has one of the fastest, hollowest left-handed waves in the world. After a three-hour surf session I was starving and headed for the nearest street stall, where I stumbled upon an old lady serving chilli octopus stuffed into a bread roll. I quickly found myself with a three-roll-a-day addiction. The sambal is inspired by that old lady, although I took away the massive chilli content to end up with this Fins favourite.

This is one of my favourite peasant-inspired dishes — another recipe that I fell in love with in Portugal. It is a wetter than usual seafood risotto.

## arroz de marisco

400 g (14 oz) skinless, boneless firm white fish fillets, such as blue-eye trevalla or kingfish
12 pipis or clams (vongole)
6 fresh bugs, slipper lobsters or scampi
6 small cleaned squid tubes
1.5 litres (52 fl oz/6 cups) fish or chicken stock (Basics, see page 230)
a pinch of saffron threads
12 large raw king prawns (shrimp), peeled and deveined, tails left intact

3 tablespoons extra virgin olive oil
2 brown onions, thinly sliced
3 garlic cloves, finely chopped
12 anchovy fillets, chopped
4 fresh bay leaves
3 tablespoons lisbon paste (Basics, see page 226)
440 g (15$^1$/$_2$ oz/2 cups) arborio rice
125 ml (4 fl oz/$^1$/$_2$ cup) dry white wine
250 g (9 oz/1 cup) tinned chopped tomatoes
80 g (2$^3$/$_4$ oz/$^1$/$_2$ cup) pitted kalamata olives, halved, to serve
2 handfuls flat-leaf (Italian) parsley, finely chopped, to serve

Serves 6

First, prepare the seafood. Cut the fish fillets into bite-sized pieces. Soak the clams or pipis in cold water for 30 minutes. Discard any broken ones or open ones that don't close when tapped on the bench. Refrigerate until needed.

Turn the bugs upside down. Insert a large knife through the shell between the legs, cutting through and along the tail and head. Slice the squid tubes in half to open and then cut each into quarters.

Put the stock in a saucepan over medium heat until it is hot, but not boiling. Reduce the heat to very low and add the saffron. Leave to infuse for 20 minutes. Bring the stock to a gentle simmer and keep hot.

Heat the oil over medium heat in a large, heavy-based saucepan. Cook the onion and garlic for 2 minutes, stirring occasionally, or until the onion is golden. Add the anchovies, bay leaves and lisbon paste and stir for 4 minutes, or until the anchovies break down. Add the rice and stir until well coated. Add the wine and stir through, then stir in the chopped tomatoes.

Reduce the heat to low and keep at a simmer. Stirring constantly, add 1.25 litres (44 fl oz/ 5 cups) hot stock, a cupful at a time, waiting until each one is almost absorbed before adding the next, until the rice is cooked but still firm to the bite — about 20–25 minutes.

Add the mussels and any remaining stock and cook for 1 minute. Add the fish pieces and bugs and cook for a further 2 minutes, stirring occasionally. Add the prawns and cook for 1 minute longer, then add the squid and keep cooking for 2–3 minutes, or until the mussels have opened and the other seafood is just cooked. Transfer to a serving dish and top with the olives and parsley.

# pan-fried fish with truffle and soy reduction

### spinach with sesame dressing

100 g ($3^1/_2$ oz/$^1/_3$ cup) tahini
$2^1/_2$ tablespoons light soy sauce
$2^1/_2$ tablespoons mirin
25 g (1 oz) sugar
$1^1/_2$ tablespoons rice wine vinegar
250 g (9 oz/ 5 cups) baby English spinach leaves

### truffle and soy reduction

125 ml (4 fl oz/$^1/_2$ cup) soy sauce
3 tablespoons vegetable oil
3 tablespoons rice wine vinegar
3 tablespoons mirin
55 g (2 oz/$^1/_4$ cup) caster (superfine) sugar
2 garlic cloves, crushed
3 cm ($1^1/_4$ inch) piece ginger, finely chopped
3 teaspoons sesame oil
3 tablespoons peanut oil
2 tablespoons lime juice
1 red banana chilli, seeded and membrane
    removed, finely chopped
1 heaped tablespoon cornflour, dissolved in
    2 teaspoons water
250 ml (9 fl oz/1 cup) pouring (whipping) cream
185 ml (6 fl oz/$^3/_4$ cup) chicken stock (Basics,
    see page 230)
1 teaspoon white truffle oil

### crisp sushi rice

200 g (7 oz/1 cup) sushi rice
3 tablespoons rice wine vinegar
2 tablespoons mirin
80 ml ($2^1/_2$ fl oz/$^1/_3$ cup) peanut oil

750 ml (26 fl oz/3 cups) dashi stock (Basics,
    see page 230)
1 large daikon, sliced into 1.5 cm ($^5/_8$ inch) thick
    slices, then cut into 5 cm (2 inch) rounds
    using a biscuit cutter
6 large fresh shimeji mushrooms, stems removed
6 x 175 g (6 oz) thick boneless white fish fillets,
    such as mahi mahi, snapper, bar cod
    or pearl perch
plain (all-purpose) flour, for dusting
80 ml ($2^1/_2$ fl oz/$^1/_3$ cup) peanut oil, for frying
2 chives, finely chopped, to garnish

Serves 6

To make the spinach with sesame dressing, whisk the tahini with the light soy sauce, mirin, sugar and vinegar. Remove the stalks from the spinach. Plunge the leaves into a saucepan of salted boiling water for 10 seconds, or until wilted. Transfer immediately to a bowl of iced water to refresh and drain well, then transfer to a bowl. Pour over the dressing and toss to combine. Set aside until needed.

To make the truffle and soy reduction, put 60 ml (2 fl oz/¼ cup) water in a large saucepan and add the soy sauce, vegetable oil, vinegar, mirin, sugar, garlic, ginger, sesame and peanut oils, lime juice and chilli. Bring to the boil, then reduce the heat and simmer for 10 minutes. Stir in the cornflour mixture until the sauce is slightly thickened, glossy and coats the back of a wooden spoon. Pass through a fine sieve. Return the strained liquid to the warm pan and add the cream, chicken stock and truffle oil. Maintain at a gentle simmer until ready to serve.

To make the sushi rice, rinse the rice under cold water until the water runs clear. Put the rice and 750 ml (26 fl oz/3 cups) water in a heavy-based saucepan, with a tight-fitting lid, over high heat. Bring to the boil and boil for 3 minutes. Lower the temperature to a gentle simmer. Cook for a further 10 minutes. Remove from the heat and stand for 10 minutes, keeping the lid on.

Transfer the rice to a large bowl and fluff the rice with a fork, then lightly stir in the vinegar and mirin. Season with sea salt. Line a tray with baking paper and spread the rice out evenly to a 2 cm (¾ inch) thickness. Press the rice down with wetted hands and refrigerate for 30 minutes, or until chilled. Cut the pressed rice into six portions using a 6 cm (2½ inch) biscuit cutter. Heat a large non-stick frying pan over medium–high heat and add the peanut oil, frying each cake for 2 minutes on each side, or until lightly golden. Keep warm in a low oven.

Put the dashi stock in a saucepan over high heat and bring to the boil. Reduce the heat, add the daikon and simmer for 15 minutes, or until the daikon is tender. Remove the daikon from the pan with a slotted spoon and set aside in a bowl. Add the shimeji mushrooms to the simmering stock in the pan for 1 minute, or until tender. Remove from the pan, place with the daikon and keep warm in a low oven.

Season the fish fillets with sea salt, then roll to lightly coat in the flour. Heat the peanut oil in a large frying pan over medium heat. Cook the fish fillets for 3 minutes on each side, or until opaque and almost cooked in the centre.

To serve, put a daikon round on each plate and sit a sushi rice cake on top. Rest the fish on top of the stack and drizzle over some of the hot truffle and soy reduction. Top with shimeji mushroom with finely chopped chives and serve with the spinach and sesame dressing on the side. A trick we use in the restaurant is to soak some Chinese cabbage (wong bok) leaves in hot water and then use the leaves to wrap up the spinach in a tight roll. We then slice the rolled spinach on the diagonal into neat pieces and serve.

## snowy's fish

200 ml (7 fl oz) extra virgin olive oil
1 brown onion, finely sliced
8 kipfler (fingerling) potatoes
24 green beans, trimmed
4 x 165 g (5³/4 oz) skinless, boneless white fish
    fillets, such as jew fish, snapper, mahi mahi
    or pearl perch
white pepper, to taste
plain (all-purpose) flour, for dusting (optional)
250 ml (9 fl oz/1 cup) riesling
55 ml (1³/4 fl oz) freshly squeezed lemon juice
2 tablespoons butter, melted
2 tablespoons chopped flat-leaf (Italian) parsley

Serves 4

This is exactly the way I like to eat my fish. If you prefer, you can serve it without the potatoes and add extra beans on the side for simple, clean, perfect food combining.

Preheat the oven to 180°C (350°F/Gas 4).

Heat 80 ml (2¹/2 fl oz/¹/3 cup) of the oil in a frying pan over medium heat and cook the onion for 10 minutes, or until golden brown and caramelised. Remove from the heat.

Boil the potatoes for 10 minutes, or until tender. Blanch the beans in a saucepan of salted boiling water for 3 minutes, or until just starting to become tender. Refresh immediately in a bowl of iced water then quickly drain. Toss the potatoes, caramelised onion and beans in 2 tablespoons of the extra virgin olive oil and season with sea salt, to taste. Cover to keep warm.

Season the fish lightly with salt and white pepper, then toss in the flour to coat, shaking off any excess.

Heat the remaining oil in an ovenproof frying pan over medium heat. Add the fish and cook for 2 minutes on each side, or until golden. Add the wine and lemon juice to the pan and brush the butter over each fish fillet. Season with sea salt, if desired. Place the pan in the oven for 3 minutes, or until the fish is almost cooked through to the centre.

When the fish is cooked, divide the potatoes and beans between each plate and arrange a fish fillet over the top. Add the parsley to the sauce and drizzle over the fish, to serve.

# fins fish

### fins paste

1/2 small white onion, finely sliced
2 garlic cloves, crushed
2 cm (3/4 inch) piece ginger, finely chopped
3 basil leaves, roughly torn
1 1/2 teaspoons kecap manis
1 1/2 teaspoons tamarind concentrate
a small handful flat-leaf (Italian) parsley, finely
    chopped
30 g (1 oz) Fins shrimp paste (Basics, see
    page 223)

### lotus root chips

100 g (3 1/2 oz) lotus root (see note)
1 tablespoon white vinegar
vegetable or cottonseed oil, for deep-frying

### coconut sambal

1 coconut, flesh finely grated
1/2 red onion, finely chopped
1/2 small tomato, seeds removed and finely
    chopped
1/2 teaspoon chilli powder
1 tablespoon freshly squeezed lime juice

### fins sauce

55 ml (1 3/4 fl oz) peanut oil
2 teaspoons sesame oil
1/2 white onion, finely sliced
1 garlic clove, finely sliced
1/2 cm (1/4 inch) piece ginger, finely sliced
1/2 small fresh red chilli, seeded and finely sliced
1 1/2 tablespoons red curry paste
2 teaspoons kecap manis
1 1/2 tablespoons fish sauce
1 1/2 tablespoons tamarind water (Basics, see
    page 231)
250 ml (9 fl oz/1 cup) chicken stock (Basics,
    see page 230)
1 lemon myrtle leaf
1/2 makrut (kaffir lime) leaf

### fins vegetables

100 ml (3 1/2 fl oz) vegetable oil
1 brown onion, finely sliced
3 garlic cloves, finely chopped
2 cm (3/4 inch) piece ginger, finely chopped
2 fresh bay leaves
1/4 teaspoon yellow mustard seeds
1/2 teaspoon curry powder
1 cinnamon stick
1/2 teaspoon ground cumin
1/4 teaspoon ground ginger
2 cardamom pods
80 g (2 3/4 oz) eggplant (aubergine), cut into
    1 cm (1/2 inch) cubes
80 g (2 3/4 oz/1/2 cup) butternut pumpkin (squash),
    cut into 1 cm (1/2 inch) cubes
100 g (3 1/2 oz/1/3 cup) tinned whole tomatoes
55 ml (1 3/4 fl oz) white vinegar
80 g (2 3/4 oz) zucchini (courgettes), cut into
    1 cm (1/2 inch) cubes
80 g (2 3/4 oz/1/2 cup) red capsicum (pepper),
    cut into 1 cm (1/2 inch) squares

6 x 150 g (7 oz) skinless, boneless fish fillets,
    such as cobia, mahi mahi, parrot fish,
    flathead or leatherjacket
125 ml (4 fl oz/1/2 cup) peanut oil
2 tablespoons sesame oil
125 g (4 1/2 oz/1 cup) plain (all-purpose) flour
3 tablespoons Asian marinade (Basics, see
    page 222)
steamed bok choy (pak choy), to serve
steamed jasmine rice, to serve

Serves 6

To make the Fins paste, put all the ingredients in a blender and blend for 5 minutes, or until smooth. Set aside until needed.

To make the lotus root chips, finely slice the lotus root into 2 mm (1/16 inch) thick rounds. Put the rounds in a bowl with 100 ml (3½ fl oz) water and the vinegar. Soak the lotus root for 15 minutes (this will bleach the lotus root and stop it from going black). Remove from the water and pat dry with paper towels.

Fill a deep-fryer or large heavy-based saucepan one-third full of oil and heat to 160°C (315°F). Deep-fry the lotus chips, in batches, for about 3 minutes each, or until lightly golden and crisp. Store any leftovers in an airtight container for up to 2 days.

To make the coconut sambal, place all the ingredients in a bowl. Use your hands to pinch the mixture together and rub the flavours into the coconut.

To make the Fins sauce, put the peanut and sesame oils in a large heavy-based saucepan over medium heat and cook the onion, garlic, ginger and chilli for 5 minutes, or until the onion has softened. Add the curry paste and cook for a further 2 minutes, stirring constantly. Add the kecap manis, fish sauce and tamarind water and simmer for 5 minutes, or until the liquid has reduced by half. Add the chicken stock, lemon myrtle and makrut leaves and bring to the boil, then reduce the heat and simmer for a further 15 minutes. Remove from the heat and allow to cool before transferring to a food processor. Quickly blend the mixture so the ingredients are fully combined but not completely smooth. Strain the sauce, return to the warm pan and keep warm over low heat.

To make the vegetables, heat the oil in a large saucepan over medium heat. Add the onion, garlic and ginger and sauté for 5 minutes, or until the onion has softened. Add the bay leaves and spices and gently cook for 5 minutes, or until aromatic. Add the eggplant, pumpkin, tomatoes and vinegar and stir well to combine. Reduce the heat, cover and cook for 5 minutes, stirring occasionally, until the eggplant and pumpkin are starting to soften. Add the zucchini to the pan with the capsicum and continue cooking for

5 minutes, or until the vegetables are tender. Season to taste, remove from the heat and keep warm until ready to serve.

Preheat the grill (broiler) to high and the oven to 190°C (375°F/Gas 5). Season the fish with sea salt, then roll in the flour to coat. Heat the mixed peanut and sesame oils in a large ovenproof frying pan over medium heat. Place the fish in the pan and cook for 1–2 minutes on each side, then transfer the fish to a lightly greased baking tray and cook in the oven for 3 minutes.

Spread one tablespoon of Fins paste on each fillet and baste with the Asian marinade. Just before you are ready to serve, heat the fish under the grill for 1 minute to warm the paste.

Use a ramekin or similar mould to plate the steamed rice at one end of a platter and top the rice with three lotus chips. Arrange the steamed bok choy in the centre of the plate and place a fish fillet, paste side up, over the top. Using a 4 cm (1½ inch) biscuit cutter, make a neat mould of the vegetables at the other end of the plate. Top the vegetables with ½ teaspoon of coconut sambal and spoon the warm sauce over the fish, to serve.

note Lotus root is the tuberous root of the lotus plant, a water plant related to the water lily and commonly used in Chinese and Indian cooking. The young roots taste like artichokes and are prized in Japan for their appearance. They are available from Asian grocery stores.

This granita flavoured with lemon myrtle and finger lime is the perfect
It is sensational on a hot summer's day.

## lemon myrtle and chardonnay granita with finger lime

185 g (6$^1$/$_2$ oz/$^3$/$_4$ cup) caster (superfine) sugar
12 lemon myrtle leaves
3 tablespoons chardonnay
3 tablespoons lime juice
6 finger limes, plus extra, to garnish

Serves 6

Put 300 ml (10$^1$/$_2$ fl oz) water in a small saucepan
over medium–high heat. Stir in the sugar until it
dissolves, then bring to the boil without stirring.
Add the lemon myrtle leaves, reduce the heat and
simmer for 4 minutes. Add the chardonnay and
simmer for a further 2 minutes. Strain the liquid
and add the lime juice, to taste.

Pour the liquid into a baking tray and place in the
freezer for at least 3 hours, scraping with a fork
every 20 minutes or so, until the ice shavings start
to look like a granita. Scrape the lime pulp from
the finger limes into the tray and fold through the
ice. Spoon into chilled glasses, to serve. Garnish
with the extra finger limes.

alate-cleanser and can be served before, during or after a meal.

This is a fantastic Thai dessert — toffee mango with black sticky rice and cardamom ice cream is a winning combination and has proved a popular dessert at Fins.

## sticky rice with mango

200 g (7 oz/1 cup) black glutinous rice
2 cinnamon sticks
1 cardamom pod
4 tablespoons shaved palm sugar (jaggery)

4 large mangoes
1 tablespoon ground cinnamon
1 teaspoon allspice
115 g (4 oz/$^1$/$_2$ cup) caster (superfine) sugar
cardamom ice cream (Basics, see page 225),
    to serve (optional)

Serves 4

Put the rice in a sieve and wash under cold running water until the water runs clear. Put the rice in a bowl, cover with water and a pinch of salt, cover with plastic wrap and soak for at least 12 hours, or overnight. Drain the rice.

Line a metal or bamboo steamer with a piece of muslin (cheesecloth). Place the cinnamon and cardamom on top of the muslin and then add the rice. Put the steamer over a saucepan or wok of boiling water, cover, and steam over low–medium heat for 50 minutes, or until the rice is tender. Replenish the pot with boiling water as necessary. Remove from the heat, transfer the rice to a large bowl and add the palm sugar, stirring through until dissolved. Set aside and allow to cool.

Meanwhile, slice the mangoes to get two plump cheeks from each fruit (you should have eight in total). Peel the skin and trim each cheek to make them flat. Using an 8 cm (3$^1$/$_4$ inch) biscuit cutter, make eight rounds from the mango cheeks and place on a tray. Combine the ground cinnamon, allspice and sugar and sprinkle over the top of each round. Place under a hot grill (broiler) for 2–3 minutes, or until the sugar has caramelised.

To serve, arrange the rice on the plate in a neat circle with an 8 cm (3$^1$/$_4$ inch) diameter. Place a mango cheek on top, then repeat with another layer of rice to create a stack. Top with a mango slice, making sure the colourful caramelised side is facing up. Serve with cardamom ice cream, if desired.

At the end of a meal this is a clean and refreshing dessert — I like it so much that I used it as my dessert at the World Gourmet Summit.

# lemon myrtle panna cotta with finger lime syrup

mild-flavoured vegetable oil, for greasing
330 ml (11¼ fl oz/1⅓ cups) milk
330 ml (11¼ fl oz/1⅓ cups) pouring (whipping) cream
4 lemon myrtle leaves, crushed
4.5 cm (1¾ inch) piece ginger, chopped
3 gelatine leaves, about 20 x 5 cm (8 x 2 inches)

### crescent tuiles

15 g (½ oz) butter
2 teaspoons honey
30 g (1 oz/¼ cup) plain (all-purpose) flour, sifted
30 g (1 oz) caster (superfine) sugar
1 egg white
a pinch ground ginger

### candied ginger

280 g (10 oz/1¼ cups) caster (superfine) sugar
5 cm (2 inch) piece ginger, finely sliced

### finger lime syrup

3 fresh finger limes
235 g (8½ oz/1 cup) caster (superfine) sugar

Makes 6

Lightly grease six 125 ml (4 fl oz/½ cup) dariole moulds with oil. To make the panna cotta, put the milk, cream, lemon myrtle leaves and ginger in a saucepan over medium–high heat and bring to just below a boil (do not boil). Remove from the heat and stand for 30 minutes to allow the flavours to infuse, then gently reheat.

Soak gelatine leaves in cold water for 5 minutes, then squeeze out the excess liquid. Stir into the milk mixture until well dissolved. Strain through a sieve and pour into the dariole moulds. Refrigerate for at least 2 hours, or until set.

Meanwhile, make the crescent tuiles. Melt the butter and honey in a saucepan over low heat. Mix the flour, sugar, egg white and ginger in a bowl. Add the butter and honey and stir to combine well. Refrigerate the mixture for 30 minutes, or until chilled.

Preheat the oven to 160°C (315°F/Gas 2–3). Lightly grease two baking trays. Draw three circles with a 6 cm (2½ inch) diameter onto each sheet of baking paper and make a crescent shape within each circle. Place the baking paper onto the tray, pencilled side down. Using a palette knife, spread the mixture to fit the crescents. Cook the tuiles for 7 minutes, or until golden. Remove from the oven and allow to cool. Repeat this process until all the tuile mixture is used up, you should make about 15 tuile biscuits in total. The crescent tuiles will last for 5 days stored in an airtight container.

To make the candied ginger, put the sliced ginger in a saucepan of water and bring to the boil, then reduce the heat and simmer for 3 minutes. Drain and then repeat this process three times. Put 235 g (8½ oz/1 cup) of the sugar and 250 ml (9 fl oz/1 cup) water into a saucepan over high heat and stir until the sugar dissolves. Bring to a boil and cook for 5 minutes. Add the blanched ginger and reduce to a simmer for 25 minutes, or until the ginger is translucent and the syrup is very thick. Strain the ginger, reserving the syrup. Spread the ginger on a baking tray and toss over the remaining sugar to coat. Leave to dry on a work surface overnight. Once dry, lift out the ginger. The ginger will keep stored for 1 month in an airtight container.

To make the finger lime syrup, remove the pulp and discard the seeds. In a bowl, pour the reserved ginger syrup over the pulp and stir through. Refrigerate for 30 minutes, or until needed.

To serve, run a knife around the top edge of the moulds and invert the panna cotta onto cold plates. With a spoon, drizzle some finger lime syrup around each panna cotta and place the candied ginger on top. Add 1–2 crescent tuiles to the side of each panna cotta.

# moroccan tasting plate

### date and orange-blossom shot

80 g (2³/₄ oz/¹/₂ cup) pitted dates
250 ml (9 fl oz/1 cup) milk
¹/₂ tablespoon ground almonds
¹/₂ teaspoon ground cinnamon
¹/₂ teaspoon orange-blossom water
pouring (whipping) cream, to garnish
ground nutmeg, to garnish
ground cinnamon, extra, to garnish

Soak the dates in 150 ml (5 fl oz) milk for 4 hours, or preferably in the refrigerator overnight. Put the dates and soaking milk in a saucepan over medium–high heat and bring to a boil. Remove from the heat and allow to cool. Transfer to a food processor and blend until smooth. Add the ground almonds, cinnamon, orange-blossom water and the remaining milk. Blend to combine. Pour the liquid into 60 ml (2 fl oz/¹/₄ cup) shot glasses. Drizzle a teaspoon of cream into each glass and sprinkle each with nutmeg and cinnamon.

### sweet potato purée

200 g (7 oz) sweet potato
2 tablespoons caster (superfine) sugar
¹/₂ teaspoon ground cinnamon
1 teaspoon ground ginger
150 g (5¹/₂ oz) plain yoghurt

Peel and chop the sweet potato into 3 cm (1¹/₄ inch) cubes. Add to a saucepan of boiling water and cook for 10–15 minutes, or until tender. Remove from the heat and drain. Allow the sweet potato to cool slightly before transferring to a food processor and blending until smooth. Pass through a fine sieve into a mixing bowl and whisk in the sugar, cinnamon, ginger and yoghurt.

### churros

125 g (4¹/₂ oz/1 cup) plain (all-purpose) flour,
    sifted, plus extra for dusting
115 g (4 oz/¹/₂ cup) vanilla sugar
1 tablespoon extra virgin olive oil
vegetable oil, for frying

Mix the flour and 1 tablespoon of vanilla sugar in a mixing bowl. Place 375 ml (13 fl oz/1½ cups) water and the olive oil in a saucepan and bring to the boil. Add the flour mixture to the boiling water and remove from the heat. Stir with a wooden spoon until the batter is smooth.

Transfer the batter to a mixing bowl, cover with plastic wrap and refrigerate for 30 minutes. Sprinkle the extra flour onto a clean work surface and roll the dough out to a 1 cm (½ inch) thickness. Divide the dough into 15 even-sized portions and roll each between the palm of your hands and the work surface to form 1 cm (½ inch) ropes of 10 cm (4 inch) lengths. Press together at the ends to create a donut shape.

Fill a deep-fryer or large heavy-based saucepan one-third full of oil and heat to 180°C (350°F). Deep-fry the churros, in batches, for about 3 minutes each, or until golden. Drain on paper towels and roll in the remaining vanilla sugar to coat on all sides.

### cinnamon meringue

2 egg whites
1 teaspoon lemon juice
100 g (3½ oz/½ cup) sugar
2 teaspoons ground cinnamon

Preheat the oven to 100°C (200°F/Gas 1–2). Line a baking tray with baking paper.

Put the egg whites and lemon juice in a mixing bowl and whisk together until soft peaks form. Continue whisking while adding 1 tablespoon of sugar at a time, making sure each tablespoon is thoroughly combined before adding more — when the peaks start to stiffen, add the cinnamon and whisk to combine.

Spoon the meringue mixture into a piping bag with a small nozzle. Working from the inside out, pipe the meringue onto the prepared tray to form five baskets, each with a 5 cm (2 inch) diameter for the base and a small raised edge. Place in the oven for 2 hours, or until crisp and the base is solid. Allow to cool on the tray. Once cold store in an airtight container. Meringues will last for 3–5 days.

### rose and pistachio ice cream

6 egg yolks
150 g (5½ oz/⅔ cup) caster (superfine) sugar
500 ml (17 fl oz/2 cups) pouring (whipping) cream
250 ml (9 fl oz/1 cup) milk
½ vanilla bean, split lengthways, seeds scraped
4 tablespoons edible dried rose petals
200 ml (7 fl oz) sugar syrup (see note, page 231)
100 g (3½ oz/¾ cup) shelled pistachio nuts, lightly toasted and roughly chopped
2 teaspoons rosewater

Serves 6

Whisk the egg yolks and sugar with electric beaters for 12 minutes, or until thick and pale.

Put the cream and milk into a heavy-based saucepan over medium–high heat. Add the vanilla bean and seeds and gradually bring just to a boil. Remove from the heat, allow to cool slightly and whisk into the yolk mix until well combined. Remove the vanilla bean.

Pour the mixture back into a clean saucepan and return to low heat. Stir constantly for about 10–12 minutes, or until the mixture thickens and coats the back of a wooden spoon. Do not allow it to boil or it will separate. Strain through a fine sieve and cool slightly; cover with plastic wrap and refrigerate until chilled.

Put the rose petals into a saucepan with the sugar syrup and slowly bring to the boil. Remove from the heat and set aside to cool.

Churn the ice cream base in an ice-cream machine. When the mixture is just starting to freeze, add the pistachios, rose petals, sugar syrup and rosewater. Continue churning and freeze according to the manufacturer's instructions.

Serve on six long tasting plates. Cut small pieces of coloured paper and sit under the shot glass at one end of the plate to prevent the glass from sliding. Serve the ice cream inside the meringue basket. Put a heaped tablespoon of sweet potato purée in the middle of the plate and balance three churros over the top. Scatter any left-over rose petals around the plate to garnish, if desired.

# quince crumble with vanilla ice cream

500 g (1 lb 2 oz/2$^1$/$_4$ cups) caster (superfine) sugar
$^1$/$_2$ lemon
1 kg (2 lb 4 oz) quince, peeled, cored and cut into
    2cm ($^3$/$_4$ inch) slices
1 cinnamon stick
1 star anise
140 g (5 oz/1 cup) roasted hazelnuts
55 g (2 oz/$^1$/$_2$ cup) ground almonds
90 g (3$^1$/$_4$ oz/1 cup) desiccated coconut
250 g (9 oz/2 cups) self-raising flour
40 g (1$^1$/$_2$ oz/$^1$/$_3$ cup) finely grated good-quality
    chocolate, such as couverture
1 teaspoon ground cinnamon
110 g (3$^3$/$_4$ oz/$^1$/$_2$ cup) raw (demerara) sugar
100 g (3$^1$/$_2$ oz) unsalted butter, chopped
1 kg (2 lb 4 oz) apples, such as golden delicious,
    cored, peeled, halved and cut into 3 mm
    ($^1$/$_8$ inch) slices
vanilla ice cream (Basics, see page 225), to serve

Serves 10

Preheat the oven to 160°C (315°F/Gas 2–3).

Put the sugar and 1 litre (35 fl oz/4 cups) water in an ovenproof saucepan over high heat and stir to dissolve the sugar. Squeeze the lemon juice and squeezed half lemon and add it to the saucepan. Cover with a lid and bring to the boil, then reduce the heat to a simmer.

Add the quince slices, cinnamon stick and star anise to the pan with the sugar syrup, cover with a sheet of silicone paper and then the lid. Put in the oven and bake for 3–4 hours, or until the quince is cooked and a ruby red colour. Remove from the oven, strain the quinces and remove the lemon, star anise and cinnamon stick. Set aside and allow to cool.

While the quince is cooking, put the hazelnuts, ground almonds, coconut, flour, chocolate, cinnamon, sugar and butter in a food processor and process until the mixture resembles breadcrumbs.

Increase the oven temperature to 180°C (350°F/Gas 4). Line a tray with baking paper. Grease ten 7 cm (2$^3$/$_4$ inch) round metal rings that are 7 cm (2$^3$/$_4$ inches) high. Line the inside of each ring with baking paper and place on the prepared tray. Place three slices of quince in the base of the ring to form a layer, then add a layer of apple and continue this layering until the stack is sitting about 1 cm ($^1$/$_2$ inch) below the rim. Bake for 8 minutes, or until the apple is tender.

Remove from the oven and sprinkle the crumble mixture to fill to the top of each ring, pressing down gently to flatten. Return to the oven and cook for a further 4 minutes, or until golden.

Remove from the oven and transfer each crumble to a plate before gently removing the ring. Drizzle with the quince liquid and serve with a scoop of vanilla ice cream on top.

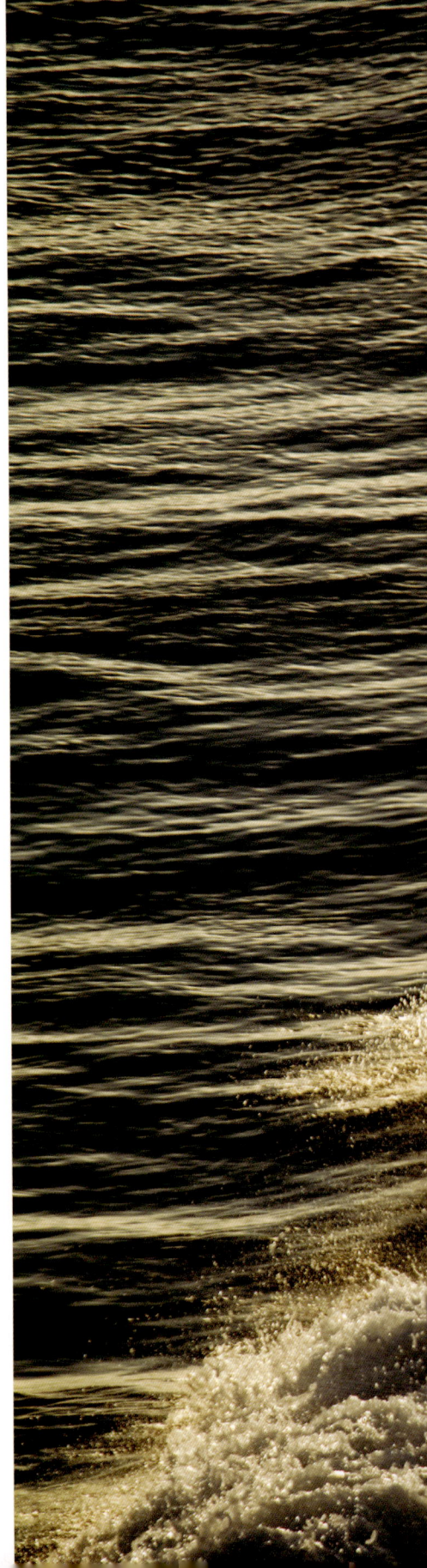

# matcha pudding

4 eggs, separated
120 g (4$^{1}$/$_{4}$ oz/heaped $^{1}$/$_{2}$ cup) caster
    (superfine) sugar
150 ml (5 fl oz) pouring (whipping) cream
100 g (3$^{1}$/$_{2}$ oz) unsalted butter, melted and cooled
    slightly
100 g (3$^{1}$/$_{2}$ oz/1 cup) sponge cake crumbs
100 g (3$^{1}$/$_{2}$ oz/$^{3}$/$_{4}$ cup) finely chopped macadamia
    nuts
1$^{1}$/$_{2}$ tablespoons matcha powder (see note)
good-quality adzuki bean ice cream, to serve
8 ready-made brandy snaps, to serve (optional)
toasted chopped macadamia nuts, to garnish

Serves 8

Preheat the oven to 180ºC (350ºF/Gas 4). Lightly
grease eight Chinese tea cups or eight holes of a
12-hole muffin tin.

Beat the egg yolks and sugar in an electric mixer
until pale and creamy. Slowly add the cream and
melted butter and continue to mix on slow until
well incorporated. Transfer the mixture to a bowl
and stir in the cake crumbs, macadamias and
matcha powder and mix well.

In a separate bowl, whisk the egg whites until
soft peaks form, then fold through the batter.
Spoon the mixture into the tea cups and place
in a deep baking dish. Pour enough hot water into
the dish to come halfway up the sides of the tea
cups. Cook in the oven for about 40 minutes,
or until a skewer inserted into the centre of the
puddings comes out clean. Run a knife around the
inside rim of each tea cup and gently turn
out each pudding onto a serving plate. Serve
with the adzuki bean ice cream and a brandy
snap, if using, and garnish with the macadamia
nuts. In the restaurant we often serve this dish
with a caramel or plum sauce.

note Matcha powder is a fine, powdered green
tea produced in Japan. It is available from most
Asian grocery stores.

# pear parfait with filo-wrapped brie and pinot syrup

### pear parfait
3 beurre bosc pears
500 ml (17 fl oz/2 cups) sugar syrup (see note, page 231)
2 teaspoons lychee liqueur (optional)
2 egg whites
90 g (3$^{1}$/$_{4}$ oz) caster (superfine) sugar
60 ml (2 fl oz/$^{1}$/$_{4}$ cup) pouring (whipping) cream

### macerated prunes
30 ml (1 fl oz) armagnac
6 prunes

### pinot syrup
250 ml (9 fl oz/1 cup) pinot noir
200 g (7 oz/1 scant cup) caster (superfine) sugar
1 star anise

### filo-wrapped brie
100 g (3$^{1}$/$_{2}$ oz/$^{2}$/$_{3}$ cup) dried figs
80 g (2$^{3}$/$_{4}$ oz/$^{1}$/$_{3}$ cup) caster (superfine) sugar
a pinch ground cinnamon
a pinch ground ginger
a small pinch ground cloves
120 g (4$^{1}$/$_{4}$ oz) good-quality brie, such as Brie de Nangis
3 sheets filo pastry
20 g ($^{3}$/$_{4}$ oz) unsalted butter, melted

Serves 6

To make the pear parfait, peel and core two of the pears and put them in a saucepan over medium heat with the sugar syrup and bring to the boil. Reduce the heat and simmer for 20 minutes, or until soft. Strain the liquid and discard. Put the pears into a food processor and blend until smooth. Add the lychee liqueur (if using) and blend briefly; the purée should have a thick consistency.

Whisk the egg whites and sugar in a large bowl until firm peaks form. In a separate bowl, whip the cream until soft peaks form.

Carefully fold the pear purée and cream together, then fold through the egg white mixture, being careful not to knock out too much air from the meringue. Spoon the mixture into six 125 ml (4 fl oz/1/2 cup) freezer-proof moulds or Chinese tea cups and freeze for at least 4 hours, or until frozen.

Meanwhile, put the armagnac and prunes in a small saucepan over medium heat and simmer for 2 minutes, or until hot. Remove from the heat and set aside for 20 minutes to cool, then refrigerate until ready to serve.

To make the pinot syrup, put the wine, sugar and star anise into a small saucepan over medium–high heat and bring to a boil. Reduce to a simmer and cook for 15 minutes, or until the liquid is syrupy. Remove the star anise and allow to cool.

To make the filo-wrapped brie, put the figs, sugar, cinnamon, ginger and cloves in a saucepan over medium heat and bring to a boil. Reduce the heat and simmer for 20 minutes, or until the figs are soft. Allow to cool slightly and purée in a blender for 5 minutes, or until smooth. Allow to cool.

Line a baking tray with baking paper. Cut the brie into six equal wedges. Brush each pastry sheet with the melted butter and cut in half lengthways. Place a portion of the cheese at the short end of each piece of pastry. Spoon a heaped teaspoon of fig purée on top of the brie. Tuck in the sides and roll up to form a neat parcel. Brush the top of each parcel with melted butter. Place on the lined baking tray and freeze for 1 hour, or until frozen. (Brie parcels can also be stored in the refrigerator for 3 days before baking.) Preheat the oven to 190°C (375°F/Gas 5). Bake in the oven for about 8 minutes, or until golden. Allow to stand for 5 minutes before serving.

Cut the remaining pear into matchsticks. Place a parfait and a brie parcel on each plate. Divide the pear matchsticks over each parfait and place a macerated prune on top of each parcel. Drizzle the pinot syrup next to the brie parcel, to serve.

If you can't decide between cheese or a 'sweet' dessert, this one allows you to have both! The pear parfait, macerated prune and pinot syrup all combine beautifully with the crispy, soft-centred brie parcel.

# chocolate chilli torte

### torte base

185 g (6$^1$/$_2$ oz/1$^1$/$_4$ cups) chopped good-quality
    dark chocolate, such as couverture (see side
    note)
125 ml (4 fl oz/$^1$/$_2$ cup) hot, freshly brewed
    espresso
150 g (5$^1$/$_2$ oz) unsalted butter, softened
80 g (2$^3$/$_4$ oz/$^1$/$_3$ cup) caster (superfine) sugar
5 eggs, separated
1 teaspoon chilli juice (see note)
$^1$/$_2$ teaspoon ground cinnamon
$^1$/$_2$ teaspoon ground cardamom
150 g (5$^1$/$_2$ oz/1$^1$/$_2$ cups) ground almonds

### chocolate chilli cream

550 g (1 lb 4 oz/3$^2$/$_3$ cups) chopped good-quality
    dark chocolate, such as couverture
1 tablespoon chilli juice (see note)
$^1$/$_2$ teaspoon ground cinnamon
$^1$/$_2$ teaspoon ground cardamom
a small pinch nutmeg
420 ml (14$^1$/$_2$ fl oz/1$^2$/$_3$ cups) pouring (whipping)
    cream

### chilli, port and espresso sauce

100 ml (3$^1$/$_2$ fl oz) espresso coffee
50 g (1$^3$/$_4$ oz/$^1$/$_4$ cup) sugar
80 ml (2$^1$/$_2$ fl oz/$^1$/$_3$ cup) port
3 cm (1$^1$/$_4$ inch) piece large red chilli , seeded and
    finely julienned

### chilli dust

25 g (1 oz/$^1$/$_4$ cup) icing (confectioners') sugar
2 small dried red chillies
$^1$/$_4$ teaspoon sweet paprika

serves 16

I am addicted to this recipe and at one stage found myself eating a slice almost every day. After visiting South America I couldn't help but think about what this chocolate torte, originally developed by Dorothy Creenaune, would taste like with chilli added. The experiment worked and this version is the result.

To make the base, grease a 28 cm (11¼ inch) spring-form cake tin and line the base and side with two separate sheets of baking paper. Preheat the oven to 170°C (325°F/Gas 3).

Put the chocolate and espresso in a saucepan over low heat and stir constantly for 5 minutes, or until the chocolate has melted and the mixture is smooth. Remove from the heat.

Meanwhile, beat the butter and sugar with electric beaters until creamy. Add the egg yolks, one at a time, beating constantly and incorporating each yolk well before adding the next. Add the chilli juice, cinnamon, cardamom and ground almonds. Add the melted chocolate mixture and stir to combine.

In a separate bowl, beat the egg whites until stiff peaks form. Fold into the chocolate mixture.

Pour the mixture into the base of the prepared cake tin and bake for 35–40 minutes, or until a skewer inserted into the centre comes out clean. Allow to cool in the tin and when cool, use your hands to press down firmly to compress the base. Set aside.

To make the chocolate chilli cream, melt the chocolate in a heatproof bowl over a saucepan of simmering water, making sure the base of the bowl does not touch the water. Remove from the heat and stir through the chilli juice. Add the dry spices to the chocolate mixture, add the cream and stir well to combine.

Gently remove the baking paper from the sides of the tin (but not from the base). Pour the chocolate chilli cream over the base and refrigerate for 3–4 hours, or until set.

Meanwhile, make the chilli, port and espresso sauce. Combine the espresso, sugar and port in a saucepan over high heat and bring to the boil. Reduce the heat and simmer for 3 minutes, or until syrupy. Add the chilli to the sauce, then remove from the heat and stand for 10 minutes for the flavours to infuse.

To make the chilli dust, combine all the ingredients in a spice grinder with a pinch of salt or grind in a mortar and pestle to form a fine powder. Sift the powder to remove any large pieces of chilli.

Cut the torte into wedges, sprinkle with the chilli dust and drizzle with a little sauce, to serve.

note To extract chilli juice, finely chop the chilli and squeeze the juice through a square of muslin (cheesecloth). To extract enough chilli juice for this recipe (1 teaspoon plus 1 tablespoon) you will need 1 banana chilli.

couverture chocolate
Whenever a recipe calls for milk chocolate, use couverture, a smooth, glossy high-grade cooking chocolate containing a minimum of 32 per cent cocoa butter. You will end up with a far better tasting product. A knob of unsalted butter, added to the saucepan when melting the chocolate, renders the finished product more flavoursome, full and glossy.

# basics

## asian marinade

70 ml (2¹/₄ fl oz) grapeseed oil
1 tablespoon sesame oil
1 cm (¹/₂ inch) piece ginger, finely chopped
1 garlic clove, crushed
1 tablespoon oyster sauce
2 tablespoons kecap manis
1 tablespoon fish sauce
red chilli, finely chopped, to taste (optional)

Makes 1 cup

Put the grapeseed and sesame oils, ginger, garlic, oyster sauce, kecap manis, fish sauce and chilli into a bowl. Stir to combine and use as required. Asian marinade can be stored, covered, in the refrigerator for up to 2 days.

## chermoula

1 tomato, finely chopped
1 small red onion, finely chopped
3 tablespoons finely chopped flat-leaf (Italian) parsley
2 tablespoons finely chopped coriander (cilantro) leaves
¹/₄ teaspoon ground saffron
1 tablespoon freshly squeezed lemon juice
2 tablespoons olive oil
1 garlic clove, finely chopped
1 teaspoon Moroccan spice (Basics, see page 226)

Makes 2 cups

To make the chermoula, mix all the ingredients together in a bowl with 1 teaspoon sea salt. If not using immediately, store the chermoula in an airtight container and cover with a layer of olive oil. It is best consumed within 2 days. Chermoula is at its best served with fish, chicken, lamb and goat, or try adding a pinch to flavour a couscous salad.

## chilli capsicum jam

**This jam is great with savoury biscuits and Turkish bread. You can alter the flavour of the jam by varying the type of chilli you use. For example, use a banana chilli for less heat, or a small fresh red chilli for a hotter flavour.**

2 teaspoons sesame oil
80 ml (2¹/₂ fl oz/¹/₃ cup) peanut oil
80 g (2³/₄ oz/¹/₃ cup) shaved palm sugar (jaggery)
3 small brown onions, chopped
80 g (2³/₄ oz) fresh small red chilli, seeded
7 cm (2³/₄ inch) piece ginger, chopped
1 large garlic bulb, peeled and chopped
6 coriander (cilantro) roots, rinsed and roughly chopped
2 red capsicums (peppers), seeded, membrane removed and roughly chopped
100 ml (3¹/₂ fl oz) fish sauce
250 ml (9 fl oz/1 cup) tamarind water (Basics, see page 231)
2 large handfuls basil leaves, torn
1 small handful mint leaves
2 tablespoons dark soy sauce

Makes 4 cups

Heat the sesame and peanut oils in a saucepan over high heat. Add the palm sugar, onion, chilli, ginger, garlic and coriander root. Cook for 10 minutes or until the onion is lightly golden, stirring constantly. Add the capsicum, fish sauce and tamarind water. Bring to the boil, then reduce the heat and simmer for a further 30 minutes, or until the capsicum is soft.

Add the basil leaves, mint leaves and soy sauce and cook for a further 5 minutes. Remove from the heat and allow to cool slightly before transferring to a food processor, then blend until smooth. Store the jam in a sterilised airtight container and keep in a cool dry place. Once opened the capsicum chilli jam will last for 1 month stored in the refrigerator.

# davidson's plum chutney

The Davidson's plum or Mullumbimby plum is native to the sub-tropical rainforests of northern New South Wales. Despite their name, the Davidson's plum is not actually related to the European plum. They have a deep dark purple skin and vibrant red flesh that has a pleasantly sour taste and are harvested during the summer months. Although they can be eaten raw, they are at their best when cooked and used in sauces, jams and chutneys. Sweet European plums can be used as a substitute. If you want to add a bit of a kick to this chutney, try adding two long red chillies with seeds in.

80 ml (2¹/₂ fl oz/¹/₃ cup) peanut oil
1 tablespoon sesame oil
1 tablespoon Fins shrimp paste (Basics, see next entry)
2 brown onions, finely sliced
3 garlic cloves, finely chopped
3 cm (1¹/₄ inch) piece ginger, finely sliced
6 coriander (cilantro) roots, rinsed and chopped
90 g (3¹/₄ oz) Davidson's plums, pitted
120 g (4¹/₄ oz) plums, pitted
60 ml (2 fl oz/¹/₄ cup) tinned plum juice
125 ml (4 fl oz/¹/₂ cup) tamarind water (Basics, see page 231)
60 ml (2 fl oz/¹/₄ cup) fish sauce
1 small handful basil leaves
1 small handful mint leaves
1 tablespoon mushroom soy sauce

Makes 3 cups

Heat the oils in a saucepan over medium–high heat. Add the shrimp paste, onion, garlic and ginger and cook for 10 minutes, or until golden. Add the coriander root and all of the pitted plums and cook for 5 minutes, stirring thoroughly. Add the plum juice, tamarind water, fish sauce and herbs. Allow to simmer for 25–30 minutes, or until the juices have almost evaporated. Add the soy sauce and stir to combine. Season to taste. Allow the mixture to cool slightly before transferring to a food processor. Blend until smooth. Store the chutney in an airtight container in the refrigerator and use within 6 weeks.

# fins shrimp paste

4 tablespoons dried shrimp
1 makrut (kaffir lime) leaf
1¹/₂ teaspoons blachan paste
¹/₂ small red onion, finely chopped
2 garlic cloves, crushed
2 red banana chillies, sliced
4 cm (1¹/₂ inch) piece ginger, finely sliced
1 tablespoon finely chopped lemongrass root
2 coriander (cilantro) roots, rinsed and chopped
3 tablespoons peanut oil

Makes 1 cup

Rehydrate the dried shrimp in a bowl of boiling water for 5 minutes. Remove the shrimp and reserve the boiling water. Cut down either side of the vein of the makrut leaf and discard the vein. Finely chop. Preheat the oven to 180°C (350°F/Gas 4).

Wrap the blachan paste in foil and dry-roast in the oven for 3 minutes, or until dry and crumbly.

Put the dried shrimp, blachan paste, onion, garlic, makrut leaf, banana chillies, ginger, lemongrass and coriander in a food processor and blend until smooth, adding a little of the water from the dried shrimp to moisten if needed to help form a thick paste.

Heat the oil in a large frying pan over medium heat and add the paste. Fry for about 20 minutes, or until fragrant. Allow to cool slightly and if not using immediately store in an airtight container in the refrigerator. Once opened the shrimp paste can be used for up to 3 weeks. Cover in a layer of oil after each use.

# green papaya salad

Green papaya contains the enzyme pepain, which is a great natural tenderiser. Marinate octopus, cuttlefish or meats in your normal marinade, but add a little green papaya before cooking. The result should be the most tender octopus ever! Do not leave the papaya in the marinade for more than a few hours as it can become so tender that it falls apart before cooking.

100 ml (3¹/₂ fl oz) vegetable oil
1 tablespoon sliced garlic
1kg (2 lb 4 oz) green papaya, julienned
1 tablespoon fried red Asian shallots
1 large handful mint leaves
1 large handful basil leaves
nam jim (Basics, see page 226)

Serves 4 as a side dish

Heat the oil in a frying pan over medium–high heat and cook the garlic and onion for 1–2 minutes, or until softened. Allow to cool.

To assemble the salad, place all the ingredients in a large bowl and toss to combine well. This salad is best prepared just before eating and tastes best at room temperature.

note If serving with the Mauritian seafood sambal on page 205, sit over a colander and allow the juices to drain off before spooning the salad into ramekins or a similar type of mould to invert onto each serving plate.

# harissa

Harissa is great served in (or as) a dip, added to soups and stew for extra flavour and also for spicing up roasted or barbecued meats.

1 red capsicum (pepper)
1 teaspoon coriander seeds
1 teaspoon cumin seeds
3 garlic cloves, chopped
¹/₂ small fresh red chilli, chopped
1 small handful mint leaves, chopped
60 ml (2 fl oz/¹/₄ cup) extra virgin olive oil

Makes 1 cup

Preheat the grill (broiler) to high. Cut the capsicum into large pieces, removing the membrane and seeds. Cook, skin side up, under the hot grill until the skin blackens and blisters. Cool in a plastic bag, then peel and roughly chop the flesh.

To make the harissa, grind the coriander and cumin seeds in a mortar, using a pestle. Put the ground spices, garlic, chilli, capsicum, mint and oil in a food processor and blend until smooth. Season with sea salt and cracked black pepper, to taste.

If not using immediately harissa can be stored in an airtight container, covered in oil, in the refrigerator for a few days.

# ice cream (cardamom)

20 green cardamom pods (see note)
500 ml (17 fl oz/2 cups) milk
200 ml (7 fl oz) pouring (whipping) cream
1 vanilla bean, split lengthways
6 egg yolks
200 g (7 oz) caster (superfine) sugar

Makes 1 litre

Gently heat the cardamom pods in a frying pan over low heat for 2 minutes, or until fragrant. Allow to cool slightly, then remove the seeds and grind to a powder in a mortar, using a pestle.

Put the cardamom powder and the milk in a clean saucepan and bring just to the boil. Remove from the heat and rest for 30 minutes to allow the flavours to infuse.

Add the cream and scrape the vanilla seeds into the pan, adding the pod as well. Bring just to the boil. Remove from the heat and set aside (do not refrigerate).

Whisk the egg yolks and sugar with electric beaters for 3 minutes, or until pale and foamy.

Pour the cream mixture into the egg mixture, stirring constantly with a wooden spoon. Return to a clean saucepan and cook over low–medium heat, stirring all the time, for 10 minutes, or until the liquid coats the back of a spoon. Do not allow it to boil or it will separate. Strain, discarding the vanilla seeds and pod, and cardamom. Cool slightly, then cover and refrigerate until cold.

Transfer to an ice-cream machine and freeze according to the manufacturer's instructions. Alternatively, put the container in the freezer, whisking every couple of hours until the ice cream is frozen and creamy in texture.

note Of all the varieties, green cardamom is superior in flavour. It is available from the spice section in most supermarkets.

# ice cream (vanilla)

6 egg yolks
200 g (7 oz) caster (superfine) sugar
580 ml (20$1/4$ fl oz/2$1/3$ cups) milk
200 ml (7 fl oz) pouring (whipping) cream
2 vanilla beans, split lengthways

Makes 1 litre

Whisk the egg yolks and sugar with electric beaters for 3 minutes, or until pale and foamy.

Put the milk and cream in a saucepan over low heat. Scrape the seeds from the vanilla beans into the pan and add the pods. Bring just to the boil, then remove from the heat and set aside for 30 minutes to allow the flavours to infuse (do not refrigerate).

Pour the cream mixture into the egg mixture, stirring constantly with a wooden spoon. Return to a clean saucepan and cook over low–medium heat, stirring all the time, for 10 minutes, or until the liquid coats the back of a spoon. Do not allow it to boil or it will separate.

Strain, discarding the vanilla bean pods. Cool slightly, then cover and refrigerate until cold.

Transfer to an ice-cream machine and freeze according to the manufacturer's instructions. Alternatively, put the container in the freezer, whisking every couple of hours until the ice cream is frozen and creamy in texture.

# lisbon paste

2 red capsicums (peppers)
1 garlic clove
3 tablespoons olive oil
a pinch smoked paprika

Makes 1 cup

Preheat the grill (broiler) to high. Cut the capsicum into large pieces, removing the membrane and seeds. Place the capsicum, skin side up, under the grill until the skin blackens and blisters. Cool in a plastic bag, then peel and roughly chop.

Put the capsicum, garlic, olive oil and paprika in a food processor and blend until smooth. Season with sea salt and cracked black pepper, to taste.

Lisbon paste can be stored in an airtight container in the refrigerator for up to 3 days.

# mediterranean marinade

185 ml (6 fl oz/³/₄ cup) olive oil
80 g (2³/₄ oz) unsalted butter
2 garlic cloves, crushed
3 tablespoons freshly squeezed lemon juice

Makes 1 cup

Combine all the ingredients in a small saucepan over low heat and gently heat until the butter has just melted. Remove from the heat and use as needed for each recipe.

# moroccan spice

**Moroccan spice is full of flavour and an essential part of making chermoula. It is also great used in stir-fries, marinades and added to yoghurt and cheese or cream-based sauces. All spices are best ground in small amounts for freshness and pungency.**

2 teaspoons cumin seeds
1 teaspoon coriander seeds
¹/₂ teaspoon fenugreek seeds
1 teaspoon ground paprika

Makes ¹/₄ cup

Preheat the oven to 150°C (300°F/Gas 2). Spread the cumin seeds, coriander seeds and fenugreek seeds evenly on a baking tray. Roast for about 5 minutes, or until you can smell the aroma of the spices. Grind in a spice grinder, or pound in a mortar, using a pestle, until fine. Add the paprika and mix all the spices together. Store in an airtight container and use within 3 days.

# nam jim

**Nam jim is the perfect complement to a variety of seafood and also works well with pork, chicken, beef and just about anything deep-fried!**

6 fresh long red chillies, seeded and finely chopped
3 garlic cloves, finely chopped
4 cm (1¹/₂ inch) piece ginger, peeled and finely chopped
3 coriander (cilantro) roots, rinsed and finely chopped
3 French shallots, finely chopped
150 g (5¹/₂ oz/1 cup) finely shaved palm sugar (jaggery)
100 ml (3¹/₂ fl oz) freshly squeezed lime juice
70 ml (2¹/₄ fl oz) fish sauce

Makes 2 cups

Crush the chilli, garlic, ginger, coriander root and French shallots in a large mortar, using a pestle. Transfer to a bowl and add the palm sugar, lime juice and fish sauce. Stir to combine. If not using immediately nam jim can be stored in an airtight container in the refrigerator for up to 5 days.

# parsley oil

50 g (1³/₄ oz/4 cups) parsley leaves
185 ml (6 fl oz/³/₄ cup) olive oil or vegetable oil

Makes 1 cup

Plunge the parsley into a saucepan of boiling water for 15 seconds. Remove and immediately refresh in a bowl of iced water for 1 minute. Drain and squeeze dry.

Put the parsley and oil in a food processor and blend until smooth. Refrigerate for 10 minutes, or until chilled. Strain the oil through a fine sieve.

Parsley oil can be stored in an airtight container in the refrigerator and is best used within 2 days of making.

note Any other soft green herb can be used instead of parsley. One of the most appealing qualities is its verdant bright green colour, so you can experiment with other herbs, such as coriander and basil.

# preserved lemons

**Preserved lemons are exotic, easily prepared at home and impart a flavour and perfume like no other — they are the next best thing to a holiday in Morocco, transforming any dish from the ho-hum to the sublime. When using them in cooking, only use the yellow zest, discarding any white pith, pulp and juice.**

**It is best to preserve lemons during autumn and spring when they are in season and have maximum aroma and juice. Any lemon worth its salt can be preserved, although having preserved a number of different varieties I can report most success with the thin-skinned Meyer lemon. I also think organic lemons give the best results. When choosing lemons for preserving, ensure you choose fully ripe, very yellow fragrant fruit with unblemished skin. In the case of store-bought lemons, wash well to remove the wax that is used to make them shiny.**

6 organic lemons
6 heaped tablespoons sea salt
500 ml (17 fl oz/2 cups) freshly squeezed
    lemon juice

Makes 6 preserved lemons

Wash and dry the lemons. Cut into quarters, stopping three-quarters of the way down to the base, ensuring the lemons are kept intact.

Stuff each lemon with a heaped teaspoon of sea salt. Pack the lemons into a large 1.5 litre (52 fl oz/ 6 cup) sterilised jar. Fill the jar with lemon juice and remaining salt to cover, ensuring there is no space left in the jar. Seal the jar and leave it to stand in a cool, dark cupboard for at least 6 weeks. The lemons are ready for use when the zest is tender.

Use lemon zest as needed, discarding any seeds and removing the white pith before use. Some people prefer to rinse the lemons lightly before adding to a dish to reduce the saltiness.

Preserved lemons should keep for 6 months unopened. Once opened they will last for up to 6 months stored in the refrigerator, so when you seal the jar it is useful to label and date it.

# preserved lemon dressing

zest of 1 preserved lemon (Basics, see above)
100 ml (3¹/₂ fl oz) extra virgin olive oil
100 ml (3¹/₂ fl oz) freshly squeezed lemon juice
sugar, to taste

makes 210 ml (7¹/₂ fl oz)

To make the preserved lemon dressing, place the lemon zest, olive oil and lemon juice in a food processor and blend until smooth. Add the sugar, to taste and mix through. Season with sea salt and white pepper, then use as directed.

# red curry paste

To make a good curry paste it always helps to understand what each ingredient is adding to the end product. It is also good to remember that the more preparation you put in at the beginning, the less pounding you will need to do. Pound each ingredient before adding the next one to get a gradual composite balance.

Always start pounding the chillies first, then add salt, as it helps to grind the chillies and all the subsequent ingredients. Galangal gives a curry its sharpness, but don't add too much to the paste or the curry will be astringent. The galangal gives length or depth on the palate. Lemongrass imparts the citrus flavour to the curry, but you have to peel off and discard the outer tough sheaths, using the white part only. Makrut (kaffir lime) leaves add zest and a floral flavour to the curry. Do not use too much or it will be bitter. Coriander (cilantro) root gives curries a sweet freshness. Rinse all dirt very well from the stem and chop before adding to the paste. Shrimp paste provides a great base, but roasting too long will make it bitter.

6 large dried red chillies
1/2 teaspoon cumin seeds
1/2 teaspoon fenugreek seeds
5 white peppercorns
8 red Asian shallots, peeled and sliced
4 cm (1 1/2 inch) piece galangal, peeled and
      chopped
2 lemongrass stalks (white part only),
      finely chopped
6 makrut (kaffir lime) leaves, stems removed,
      finely chopped
1 tablespoon chopped coriander (cilantro) root
2 garlic cloves, finely sliced
1 teaspoon Fins shrimp paste, wrapped in foil
      and softened under a grill (broiler) (Basics,
      see page 223)
1 teaspoon rice flour
2 tablespoons Thai basil leaves
250 ml (9 fl oz/1 cup) vegetable oil

Makes 1 cup

Soak the chillies overnight. Reserve 3 tablespoons of the soaking water, discarding the rest and remove the seeds from the chillies.

Put the cumin and fenugreek seeds in a dry frying pan over medium heat and cook for about 2 minutes, or until fragrant. Remove from the heat and grind to a fine powder in a mortar, using a pestle. Set aside until needed.

Put the chillies and chilli water in a large mortar with 1 teaspoon of sea salt and grind to a paste. Add the peppercorns, shallots, galangal, lemongrass, makrut leaves, coriander root, garlic, shrimp paste, rice flour, basil leaves and combined cumin and fenugreek powder and continue to pound, making sure you grind each ingredient before adding the next. The paste should be as smooth as possible.

Heat the vegetable oil in a wok or frying pan over medium heat, add the chilli mixture and cook for 30 minutes, stirring regularly. Aroma is the best indicator for judging a curry paste. By the end of the process it should smell integrated rather than a disparate blend of raw ingredients.

note The ingredients used to make this red curry paste will create more paste than needed for an individual dish. This is because a certain volume is required to get the balance right. Any left-over paste can be stored for 2 weeks, covered with oil, in an airtight jar in the refrigerator. Do not freeze a curry paste; when thawed the shallots and garlic become bitter and the paste loses its freshness and pungency.

# rice pilaf

100 ml (3¹/₂ fl oz) extra virgin olive oil
1 brown onion, finely sliced
1 garlic clove, finely sliced
500 g (1 lb 2 oz/2¹/₂ cups) basmati rice
125 ml (4 fl oz/¹/₂ cup) dry white wine
1 fresh bay leaf
1 teaspoon saffron powder or tumeric
400 ml (14 fl oz) warm chicken stock (Basics,
    see page 230)

Serves 8

Heat the oil in a large saucepan over high heat and sauté the onion and garlic for 10 minutes, or until golden. Add the rice to the pan and stir to coat in the oil. Add the wine and stir until the liquid has been absorbed into the rice.  Add the bay leaf, saffron powder, stock and season to taste with sea salt. Reduce the heat to low, cover, and simmer for 15 minutes, or until the rice is tender. Remove from the heat, stir and serve.

# saffron mayonnaise

8 saffron threads
1 egg yolk
1 teaspoon dijon mustard
100 ml (3¹/₂ fl oz) vegetable oil
100 ml (3¹/₂ fl oz) extra virgin olive oil
1 tablespoon white wine vinegar

Makes 1 cup

Simmer 100 ml (3¹/₂ fl oz) water and the saffron threads in a saucepan over low heat for 20 minutes, or until about 2 teaspoons of liquid remains. Set aside and allow the flavours to infuse for 20 minutes.

Put the egg yolk and dijon mustard in a blender and blend until smooth. Combine the vegetable oil and extra virgin olive oil and, with the motor still running, slowly drizzle in the oils until it is all used up and you have a thick, creamy mayonnaise. Mix in the saffron water and vinegar. Season to taste with sea salt and refrigerate until needed.

Saffron mayonnaise can be stored in an airtight container for up to 5 days.

# seaweed salad

**Like many things green, seaweed is a great natural tonic. Apart from the interesting flavours and textures it adds to a dish, seaweed offers a variety of health benefits and endless possibilities in the kitchen. Seaweed, or sea vegetable as it is known in other parts of the world, has a high mineral concentration, containing magnesium, calcium, iron, copper, potassium, zinc and natural sea salt. It also contains protein, vitamins B and C, and betacarotene, an antioxidant that may help in cancer prevention.**

3 tablespoons dried wakame
3 tablespoons mirin
1 tablespoon light soy sauce
1 tablespoon freshly squeezed lemon juice
1 tablespoon peanut oil
1 teaspoon sesame oil
2 cm (3/4 inch) piece ginger, julienned
¹/₂ red banana chilli, seeded and julienned

Serves 4–6 as a side salad

Put the wakame in a non-metallic bowl, cover with cold water and allow to stand for 5 minutes. Drain, discarding the soaking liquid.

Put the mirin, soy sauce, lemon juice, peanut and sesame oils in a non-metallic bowl and stir to combine. Add the wakame, ginger and chilli and mix together. Cover and refrigerate until needed.

## stock — chicken

5 free-range chicken carcasses, rinsed
1 white onion, chopped
5 garlic cloves, crushed
1 carrot, chopped
1 leek, white part only, chopped
10 parsley stalks
1 fresh bay leaf

Makes 8 cups

Put the cleaned chicken carcasses, onion, garlic, carrot, leek, parsley and bay leaf into a large stockpot. Add 5 litres (175 fl oz/20 cups) water and bring to the boil over medium–high heat. Reduce the heat and leave on a gentle simmer for 2 hours with the lid off, frequently skimming any scum that rises to the surface.

Remove the solids from the stock and strain through a fine sieve lined with muslin (cheesecloth). Allow to cool and if not using immediately store in the refrigerator. Remove any fat from the top before use. Chicken stock will last for 2–3 days in the refrigerator and can be stored in the freezer for up to 1 month.

## stock — dashi

5 cm (2 inch) piece kombu (see note)
25 g (1 oz/2 cups) dried bonito flakes (see note)
2 cm (3/4 inch) piece ginger, peeled and sliced
100 ml (3½ fl oz) mirin
250 ml (9 fl oz/1 cup) soy sauce

Makes 2.25 litres

Soak the kombu in a saucepan with 2 litres (70 fl oz/8 cups) water for 5 minutes. Place the saucepan over high heat and bring to the boil. Remove from the heat and add the bonito flakes. When the bonito has sunk to the bottom of the pan, strain into a clean saucepan. Bring the stock to a simmer and stir in the ginger, mirin and soy sauce. Remove from the heat, strain and use as required. Dashi stock will store for 2 days, covered, in the refrigerator.

note Kombu (a thick kelp) and bonito flakes (dried fish) are both used to flavour Japanese broths and are available from Asian grocery stores.

## stock — fish

2 kg (4 lb 8 oz) white fish skeletons
2 carrots, roughly chopped
1 large brown onion, quartered
2 garlic cloves, crushed
2 fresh bay leaves
1 large handful fresh flat-leaf (Italian) parsley

Makes 8 cups

Wash the fish skeletons under cold water, then place in a large stockpot or saucepan. Add all the ingredients and 3 litres (105 fl oz/12 cups) water. Bring to the boil, reduce the heat and simmer for 20 minutes. Strain the stock, discarding the fish and vegetables. Season with sea salt and cracked black pepper, and use as directed.

Fish stock needs to be used within 2 days or it will not taste fresh. If you are not using it immediately, cover and store in the refrigerator. It can be frozen for up to 1 month.

## stock — master

1 litre (35 fl oz/4 cups) chicken stock (Basics, see left)
125 ml (4 fl oz/1/2 cup) dark soy sauce
125 ml (4 fl oz/1/2 cup) light soy sauce
125 ml (4 fl oz/1/2 cup) shaoxing rice wine
20 g (3/4 oz) Chinese rock sugar
1 star anise
1 cinnamon stick
1 teaspoon fennel seeds
1 teaspoon sichuan peppercorns
6 cardamom pods
4 cm (1½ inch) piece dried orange peel
1 small fresh red chilli, sliced
3 cm (1¼ inch) piece ginger, peeled and sliced
3 cm (1¼ inch) piece fresh galangal, sliced
1 piece of dried liquorice root

Makes 4 cups

Place all ingredients into a large saucepan over medium–high heat. Bring to the boil, then reduce to a simmer and gently cook for 3 hours. Strain and discard the solids, reserving the liquid. Store after each use in an airtight container in the refrigerator — you can add new ingredients to it each time you use it.

# sugar syrup

440 g (15½ oz/2 cups) caster (superfine) sugar

Makes 3 cups

Put the sugar and 500 ml (17 fl oz/2 cups) water in a saucepan over high heat and slowly bring to the boil, stirring to dissolve the sugar. Boil for about 5 minutes, then remove from the heat and allow to cool before using as directed.

# tamarind dressing

100 ml (3½ fl oz) tamarind water (Basics, see below)
1½ tablespoons mirin
2 teaspoons freshly squeezed lemon juice

Makes ¼ cup

Put the tamarind water, mirin and lemon juice in a saucepan over high heat and stir to combine. Reduce the heat and simmer for 15 minutes, or until the liquid thickens to a coating consistency. Use as directed.

# tamarind water

To make tamarind water, put the tamarind pulp in the same quantity of water and allow to stand for 1 hour, then break up with a spoon. Then strain and discard the pulp. For example, if you need 100 ml (3½ fl oz) tamarind water, use 100 g (3½ oz) tamarind pulp in 100 ml (3½ fl oz) water.

# tempura batter

250 ml (9 fl oz/1 cup) ice water
175 g (6 oz/1 cup) rice flour

Makes 2 cups

Put the ice water and flour in a bowl and mix together lightly with chopsticks. Do not worry if there are lumps. The colder the batter is the crispier the end result will be once fried, so it is best to work quickly once you have prepared the batter and deep-fry immediately.

note If making tempura batter for crispy oysters with wasabi pickled ginger you can add a pinch of finely ground sichuan peppercorns to the batter. If preparing the batter for the mud crab tempura you can add 1 finely chopped long red chilli, making sure you remove the seeds.

# tomato sauce

60 ml (2 fl oz/¼ cup) olive oil
1 brown onion, finely sliced
3 garlic cloves, crushed
300 g (10½ oz/1¼ cups) tinned chopped tomatoes
1 red capsicum (pepper), seeded, membrane removed and roughly chopped
1 fresh bay leaf
125 ml (4 fl oz/½ cup) dry white wine
6 drops Tabasco sauce

Makes 2½ cups

To make the tomato sauce, heat the olive oil in a saucepan over medium heat. Add the onion and cook for 5 minutes, or until soft. Add the garlic and cook for a further 3 minutes. Add the tomato and capsicum and cook for 5 minutes, or until the capsicum has softened slightly. Add the bay leaf and wine, bring to the boil, then reduce to a simmer and cook for 20 minutes, or until slightly pulpy. Add the Tabasco sauce. Remove from the heat and allow to cool slightly. Remove the bay leaf and blend in a food processor until smooth. Season with sea salt and cracked black pepper, to taste. Return to a clean saucepan and keep warm until needed.

If you are not using the sauce immediately, store, covered, in the refrigerator for up to 5 days.

## turmeric pickle

**Serve turmeric pickle as an accompaniment to fried fish, chicken or pork. It is also great with Thai-style green papaya or mango salads. It can be used with squid or cuttlefish and grilled on a barbecue as well.**

200 g (7 oz) fresh turmeric, finely sliced
220 g (7³/4 oz/1 cup) sugar
1 fresh long red chilli, finely sliced
3 cm (1¹/4 inch) piece ginger, finely sliced
1 tablespoon fish sauce
150 ml (5 fl oz) rice wine vinegar

Makes 2¹/2 cups

To avoid an earthy taste, blanch the turmeric three times in a saucepan of boiling water for 10–15 seconds each time, plunging into iced water afterwards before draining well. Peel and finely slice — use gloves before you start handling the turmeric to prevent staining.

Make a sugar syrup by putting the sugar and 250 ml (9 fl oz/1 cup) water in a saucepan over medium heat and stirring until the sugar has dissolved and the liquid is clear. Add the turmeric, bring almost to the boil, then reduce the heat and simmer for 5 minutes.

Add the chilli, ginger, fish sauce and vinegar and simmer for a further 5 minutes. Allow to cool. Place the cooled pickle into a sterilised airtight jar and store in the refrigerator until ready to use. The turmeric pickle will store for 1 week in the refrigerator once opened.

note Fresh turmeric stores well for up to 1 week when kept dry in the refrigerator. Wrap it in a paper towel and then seal in plastic wrap.

## yuzu mayonnaise

**Yuzu is a yellow citrus fruit from Japan, about the size of a tangerine and quite sour — it is grown mainly for its zest. Yuzu paste sometimes contains chilli, which adds a kick to its pungent flavour. It is available at Asian grocery stores. If you have trouble finding it you can substitute 1 teaspoon fresh lime juice and 1 teaspoon lime zest, instead.**

2 egg yolks
1 tablespoon yuzu paste
3 tablespoons freshly squeezed lemon juice
40 g (1¹/2 oz) caster (superfine) sugar
200 ml (7 fl oz) vegetable oil
chilli powder, to taste

Makes 1¹/4 cups

Put the egg yolks, yuzu paste, lemon juice and sugar into a food processor. Blend to combine. With the food processor still going, slowly drizzle in the oil. Blend until all the oil is added and a thick mayonnaise consistency is achieved. Season with the chilli powder and sea salt, to taste. Yuzu mayonnaise can be stored in the refrigerator, covered, for up to 3 days.

index

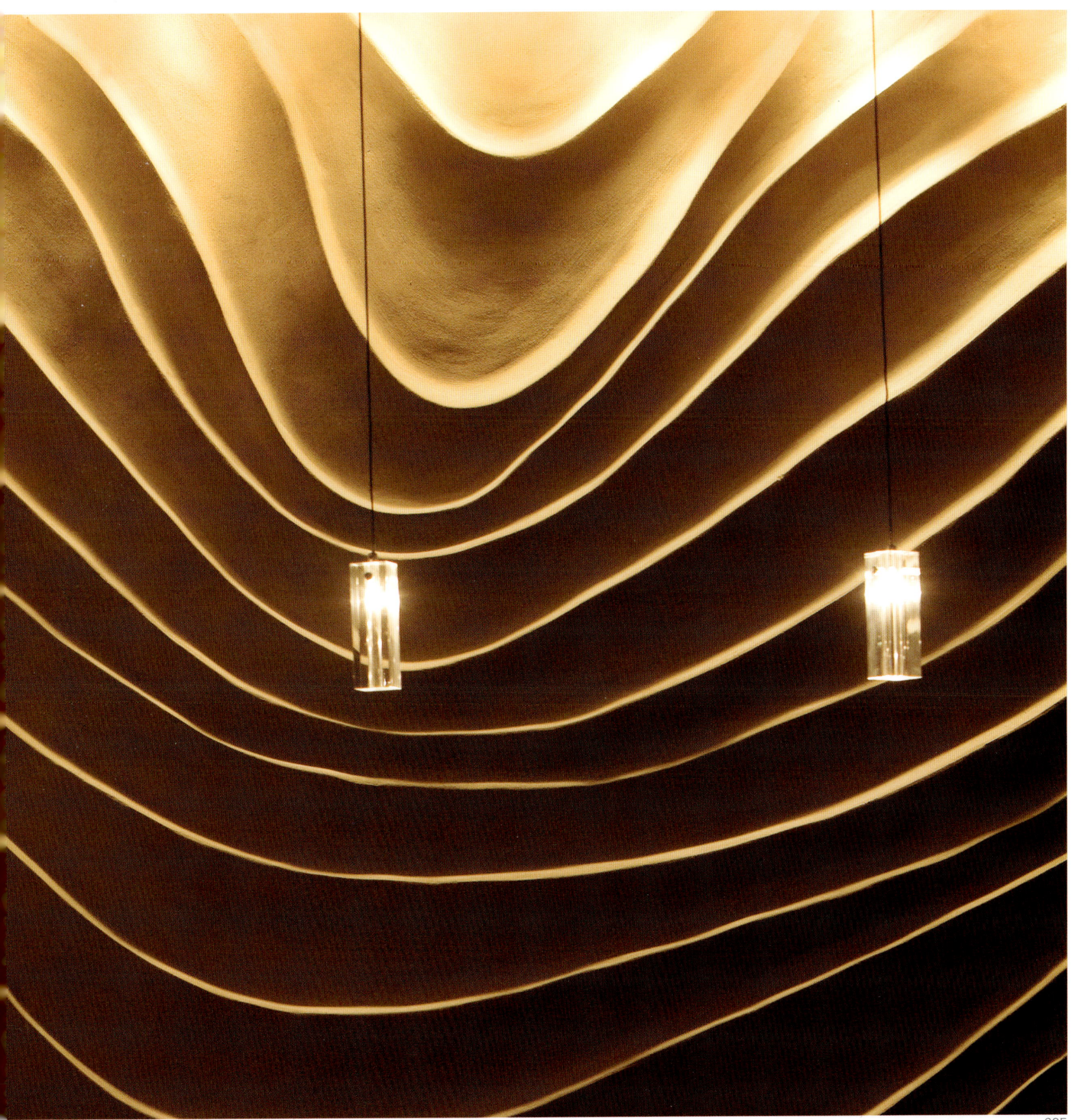

## ACKNOWLEDGMENTS

Firstly, I would like to thank the Fins clientele who have supported us through each incarnation of the restaurant. Some have been to all three!

**Thanks also to my wonderful wife Morgan — an amazing talent who always found time to ask the right questions as I worked on the book and simultaneously managed the restaurant, walked on the beach and painted portraits! I hope she stays at Fins even after winning the Archibald.**

Margarida, a big thank you for many great years, introducing me to Portugal, and helping to start Fins; as well as my Portuguese family for fostering my continuing love of Portugal.

**While I am responsible for the philosophy and ideas in Fins kitchen I greatly thank every chef I have worked with.**

A good kitchen is a start but nothing without great service. Fortuitously, I have had some of the best waiter and sommelier talent over many years at Fins. Thank you guys.

**I am absolutely excited by fresh fish and seafood. I must thank Freckle from Bay Seafood, Ted from Brunswick Co-op, and all the local fishermen for the 6 am wake-up calls.**

I love finger limes and Judy and Ash Viola have been generous, knowledgeable and inspirational.

**Marco from MC Design has given me a great space to work while our customers celebrate his design in the bar and dining room.**

The team at Murdoch Books is the best — thanks to Juliet Rogers, Kay Scarlett and Jane Lawson for bringing the first edition to life. Thanks to Jacqueline Blanchard, my editor, who kicked and prodded at all the right times, and MaryLouise Brammer for the great design. Thanks also to Kylie Walker, Desney King, Gabriella Sterio and Tania Gomes who worked on the revised edition of the book.

**Most importantly, thank you to the local fish, prawns, squid, bugs and octopus for making this book possible.**